STORIES OF INNS
AND THEIR SIGNS

ALSO BY ERIC R. DELDERFIELD

British Inn Signs and Their Stories
Introduction to Inn Signs
Church Furniture
Kings and Queens of England and Great Britain
Eric Delderfield's Book of True Animal Stories
(2 vols)
West Country Historic Houses and Their
Families (3 vols)

The sign of the *Gupshill Manor*, the fourteenth century inn at Tewkesbury (Glos). Associated with many of the great events in England's history. Queen Margaret, wife of Henry VI, spent the night before the last battle of the Wars of the Roses at the inn. From the windows she could see the 'Bloody Meadow' where the battle was fought.

STORIES OF INNS
AND THEIR SIGNS

ERIC R. DELDERFIELD

DAVID & CHARLES

NEWTON ABBOT   LONDON
NORTH POMFRET (VT) VANCOUVER

0 7153 6249 6

Set in 10 point Plantin
and printed in Great Britain
by Taylor Brothers (Bristol) Limited
Published in the United States of America
by David & Charles Inc North Pomfret
Vermont 05053 USA
Published in Canada by Douglas David &
Charles Limited 3645 McKechnie Drive
West Vancouver BC

CONTENTS

PREFACE - - -- - - - 9

PART 1. STORIES OF INNS - - 11–61

PART 2. CATEGORIES OF SIGNS - 62–90

    Religious - - - - 62
    Royal and Heraldic - - - 62
    Politicians and Others - - 64
    Travel and Transport - - 66
    Naval and Military - - - 70
    Trades and Callings - - - 74
    Agricultural and Countryside - 76
    Animals, Birds, Fish and Reptiles 76
    Traditional and Local Associa-
       tions - - - - - 80
    Sporting - - - - 82
    Humorous and Punning Signs - 84
    Nursery Rhymes - - - 84
    Musical Instruments - - 84
    The World of Literature - - 84
    Not What They Seem - - 85
    Largest and Smallest - - 87
    Some New Names and Modern
       Buildings - - - - 87
    And Still They Come - - 90

PART 3. AND ASSOCIATED WITH
      INNS - - - - 91–99

    The Story of the Cogers - - 91
    The British Pub Invades the
      Continent and the New World 92
    The Sign Painters - - - 95

ACKNOWLEDGEMENTS - - - 100

GENERAL INDEX - - - 101–105

INDEX OF INNS - - - 106–112

PREFACE

Where there is an inn there is invariably a story. With some, it may be a claim to historical associations, others may have been frequented by famous people, and a great many acquired the name on their signboard under strange circumstances. It can be a fascinating quest to try and trace the story behind a curious name and he would be a dullard indeed who failed to be interested in the origin of the names of such inns as the *Land of Liberty*, the *Busby Stoop*, the *Donkey & Buskins*, the *Dairy Maid* or the *Roundstone*. And even without the inns to which they gave their names, stories such as those of that weird contraption the 'Impulsoria', the 'Atmospheric' railway experiment, or the smuggling fraternity of the seventeenth century in Sussex are all well worth the telling.

The origins of 'Innsignia' go far back into English history and the foreign visitor's delight in this peculiarly British tradition is understandable when one recalls that the grand old galleried *New Inn*, in Gloucester (Glos), for instance, was already forty years old when Columbus discovered America. There is scarcely a subject—be it monarch, famous or infamous person, animal, bird, reptile or event—which has not given its name to an inn, and though some may be simply frivolous, such as the *Duke Without a Head,* most of the names have stories to tell.

Another curious feature of British inns is the way in which their numbers vary from town to town. Some quite small places have a surprising number to serve their modest populations, and this is often a sign of a once thriving community —perhaps an old mining town, or a once busy inland port—whose prosperity has receded, though the inns have somehow managed to keep going. A good example is the town of Cockermouth (Cumb). Today it has a population of around 5,000 and though many of its inns have disappeared over the years, still to be found in the main street, almost next door to each other, are the *Globe,* the *Black Bush,* the *Brown Cow,* the *Apple Tree* and the *Bush.* Just across the street is the *Trout,* and these are not all of them. Whitehaven, another of Cumberland's old towns, was once famed for the great coalmines owned by the Lonsdale family, which ran under

the sea. Here, too, are a large number of inns, including several such as the *Paul Jones* and the *Distressed Sailors* which have associations with the town's history.

In Devon, halfway up the river Exe, lies the little town of Topsham, once a busy shipbuilding centre and port. Today its population has dwindled to some 3,500 but the town still boasts a dozen inns, most of them with nautical associations and names. And Starcross, on the opposite side of the river has four inns to serve a population of 1,000.

Inns have played many roles over and above their primary function and hardly an aspect of community living has not had some association with the British inn. They have been meeting places for guilds and societies, provided rooms for coroners' inquests, been the scene of auctions, and in a thousand other ways provided community services. Even today at a Somerset village inn, a surgery is held by three doctors in the licensee's sitting-room and the lounge bar is the waiting-room. At a village in Kent, an inn also serves as a sub-post office.

Another important role of the inn in days gone by was to serve as a 'signpost' or landmark. Prior to the introduction of street numbering, the inn with its prominent sign was the ideal landmark from which to give directions, for every local inhabitant was familiar with its whereabouts. The alternative was as given in advertisements for the first Haymarket theatre in London, in which theatregoers of 1703 were informed that they could find it by 'the second stableyard on the left going up the Haymarket'.

In 1797 all signs which projected across the street were made illegal, though innkeepers were still obliged to display a sign on their premises. Today, in the planner's world in which we live, local authority permission has to be sought before any swinging or projecting sign may be displayed and when recently a sign advertising the *Artichoke,* Christow (Devon), was refused by the county council appeal had to be made to the Department of the Environment in London to get the refusal overruled.

Canal, railway and coach transport are featured on many inn signs throughout the country but the 'Hansom Cab' or the 'Growler' seem to have been missed. Motoring, too, has its *Bullnose Morris*, and air transport its *Comet* and *Walrus*, but as yet there does not seem to be a 'Hovercraft', or a 'Concorde'.

Dozens of inns bear the names of campaigns and battles of long ago, but so far there is no 'Alamein' or 'Battle of Britain'. Nor is there a 'Dam buster', a 'Guy Gibson', or a 'Douglas Bader', each of whom became as much legends in our time as did General Rawdon (1604-84) or Admiral Vernon (1684-1757), after whom inns have been named. A few soldiers and sailors of World War II, including General Cunningham, have been similarly commemorated but they are few indeed compared with the crops produced by earlier wars.

Some inn signs bearing people's names defy all attempts to discover why those particular individuals received the inn sign 'accolade'—such as *Lord Westbury*, Wandsworth (London), or *Sir William Gomm*, London, SE16—when they appear to have had no connection with the towns or districts concerned. Yet this is frequently the case.

Many trades and livery companies have somewhere an inn named after them, but there are a number of curious omissions. Where for instance are the pewterer's arms, or those of the upholders, tallow-chandlers, scriveners, loriners, horners, upholsterers, joiners and ceilers, furniture makers, gold and silver wyre drawers, clockmakers, tanmakers, basketmakers or innholders? All these have their livery companies but apparently no inn has yet been named after any one of them.

One of the few remaining 'beam' signs which span the road still is that of the *Magpie*, Stonham, nr Ipswich (Suffolk). Known affectionately as the 'Stonham Pie' inn, it had until recent years a magpie in a cage at the entrance. Only about a dozen of these 'gallows' signs which once enlivened the countryside now remain.

Most areas have signs of special local association, as for instance, the Cotswolds with its *Lamb, Fleece*, etc but alas, not all the inns mentioned in these pages have a sign. The south is more sign conscious than the north, which is regrettable as so many North Country names are worth illustrating.

Of my two previous books on the subject of British inn signs, the first, 'British Inn Signs and their Stories,' developed from the interest shown in two small booklets published in 1961-62. The second book, 'Introduction to Inn Signs', was planned to meet the demand for an abridged edition of the first book. In this, my third volume, the emphasis has been reversed and stories associated with inns take pride of place over signs as such, though naturally some signs are mentioned without stories. Care has been taken to avoid names and signs which have been mentioned in my previous books, although where new information has since come to hand, or a name is necessary to illustrate a point, a few have been mentioned for the second time. I have already recorded many of the better-known stories concerning inns and these have not, therefore, been repeated here.

Included in this volume are lists of signs, in their various categories, which have come to me since my two previous books were published. The subject, however, is a never-ending one and whilst every effort has been made to bring the lists up to date, it must be remembered that old inns are continually closing or undergoing a change of name, and new ones are being opened. It is a continuing process among the 70,000 odd inns in the country, and while it is good to see new names replacing the more mundane ones, such as 'Railway' or 'New Inn', it is my fervent hope that those with historical associations or of specific meaning will be let well alone.

Perhaps this is the place to note that throughout this book every place has been deemed an inn. Some, of course, now claim and indeed have attained hotel status, but since from earliest days the function of an inn has been to serve travellers, and in so doing they have built up an honoured tradition, I feel that none will quarrel with my generalisation.

Every care has been taken with detail but despite checking and rechecking, some errors are almost bound to have occurred. If so, my sincere apologies.

Again, my grateful thanks to a host of regular correspondents and 'informers'. For ten years now, never a day has passed without someone either requesting or supplying information about inn signs, not only in these islands but from all over the world. I am always pleased to help with queries if I can, and odd names or stories of inns that are sent to me are always welcome.

I am indebted also to the librarians and their staffs all over Britain who so often take endless trouble on my behalf. My thanks also to the signboard artists, a rare breed of men, and to the brewers and licensees, too.

E.R.D.

Penshurst, Exmouth
September 1973

PART I

Stories of Inns

A most unusual name for an inn—at least to the southerner—is the *Yuticks' Nest*, Blackburn (Lancs) and it is a good example of the application of local usage and wit to inn signs. The inn now bearing this name was a cottage in 1862. The following year it became a beer house and later, extended, became known as the *Brickmakers' Arms* because of the number of brickfields in the vicinity. About 1875 it was taken over by a man called John Fish, who was a 'drawer-in' and whose three sons followed the same trade at local mills. Their work consisted of threading a beam through reeds before fitting it to a loom for weaving.

The 'utick' or yutick was the old Lancashire name for the whinchat which normally migrates to England in mid-April. It builds its nest on the ground and spends a good deal of its time in what appears to be a sitting posture. This was something the 'drawers-in' had in common, for they had to sit on low stools for a greater part of their working day. So it had to come about that a wit should dub the men who did this job 'uticks', the 'Y' probably being added by dialect.

As the inn was well patronised by others following the same trade as the Fish family, it was decided to change its name from *Brickmakers' Arms* to the present one.

It is a name which has aroused much curiosity over the years and two sceptical West Country people who thought the yutick was a bird similar to the extinct dodo, once wrote to the editor of a daily newspaper asking for clarification. The reply was: 'No can Dodo, friend!' So, far from being extinct, the yutick is very much alive and has its nest in Blackburn (Lancs).

At the village of Layer-de-la-Haye (Essex) there is an inn with the unique name of the *Donkey & Buskins*. Buskins were leather leggings, or gaiters, worn by farm workers and the sign shows a boy standing beside a donkey which is wearing the buskins. There are at least two theories as to how the name came about. One tale is that a farmer called at the inn one night and imbibed rather too freely. When he left, instead of replacing the buskins on his own legs, he tied them to the legs of his donkey. Pleased with the effect he obtained another pair for the animal's hind legs and with some satisfaction pronounced: 'There— the donkey in buskins!' Naturally the incident became a local joke and the inn was so named.

Another story is that a local man whose son went to the Bluecoat School at Colchester, three miles away, made the journey by donkey and, to protect the beast's legs from the thorns and thistles on Tiptree heath, he fitted the donkey with buskins.

After which it comes as something of an anti-climax to find that the 'locals' call the place the 'Dickey'.

Blanchland is a remote village in the Derwent valley near Hexham (Northumberland). It takes its name from a monastery which, founded in the twelfth century, met its end in the aftermath of the Dissolution in 1539.

There is much to remind the visitor of the abbey buildings, not least the *Lord Crewe Arms*, once part of the kitchens and abbot's guesthouse. For some years it served as the manor house and is now a fascinating inn with walls 3ft thick, a priest's hole and not one, but two ghosts.

In earlier days the village and abbey were under continual threat from border raiders and on one occasion a thick mist descended on the valley, screening the village from a marauding band then at large. The Scots gave up and were groping their way back to the border when they heard the sound of bells which the monks of the abbey were rashly pealing in thanksgiving for their deliverance. Guided by the bells, the raiders returned and, after killing every monk, pillaged the place and made off. Not surprisingly, then, that a phantom monk still returns sorrowfully to the village, perhaps in penance for having once been too hasty.

Another ghost attached to the inn is that of a pretty girl who has been trying for more than 250 years to deliver a message. Dorothy Forster was a member of the family who once lived in the former abbot's lodging. Her brother Tom, an active Jacobite in the 1715 rising, was captured and imprisoned in the Tower of London. Bravely, Dorothy rode to London, rescued him, and together they returned to Blanchland, where he was concealed in a secret room constructed in the walls. After lying low for a time, Tom was smuggled out and escaped to France. There remains the mystery of why, after so successful an adventure, the poor maiden still tries to attract the attention of visitors sleeping in her bedroom, for many bear witness to the fact that she has appeared and behaves as if she wishes to deliver a message.

The haunted bedroom is approached by a massive, black, arched door, which surmounts a flight of wide stone steps. Some visitors say they have been disturbed in the night by Dorothy, while others claim to have seen her sitting in pensive mood by the bedroom window.

The great fireplace, under which was the entrance to the secret hiding-place where Tom was successfully concealed, remains to this day and, like the intriguing bar in what was once the monastery crypt, is among the many attractions which, ghostly residents notwithstanding, draw visitors to this ancient inn. Many of them come from overseas to sample its hospitality and to meet Dorothy.

All kinds of theories have been advanced as to the meaning of the *Wig & Fidgett*, Boxted, Colchester (Essex). By far the most plausible is that the words stem from old English: wig—whicken, an old form for white, and fitchet—a polecat. Thus 'white polecat', which is yet another addition to the never-ending list of animals on inn signs.

Near Haworth (Yorks) is the *Hurlers*, recalling the ancient game in which the players had to hurl a bowl-shaped stone down a measured length of road, usually about five miles. The stone had a bias on one side and the skilful player used this to advantage to negotiate bends. The winner was the competitor who took the least number of 'hurls' to cover the distance.

A splendid example of an historical event perpetuated by the name of an inn is the *Land of Liberty*, Swillett, Chorley Wood (Herts). The story dates back to 1846 when an Irishman, Fergus O'Connor, was a prominent Chartist leader. He had long been an advocate of peasant proprietorship and, in 1846, founded the National Land Company to buy estates and form a co-operative with the object of settling members of the industrial class upon the land. The society was to consist of any number of shareholders, who could purchase

fifty-shilling shares which could be subscribed for in amounts of 3d, 6d or 1s until the full price had been paid.

The scheme was enthusiastically received by the Chartists and in no time at all over £100,000 had been subscribed. With the money, O'Connor began to search for five estates and shortly settled on Herringsgate Farm, Rickmansworth (Herts), as the first. It comprised 103 acres and work commenced to make it suitable for the purpose in view. Four roadways were built and named Halifax, Bradford, Nottingham and Stockport roads. The estate was then divided into eighteen plots of two acres, five of three and thirteen of four acres. A plot of two acres was reserved for a school. When all was ready for the official opening in August 1847, the new settlers arrived and, headed by a procession of farm carts and a band, were led to their 'promised land'.

Having settled in, the pioneers were then treated to a spate of advice on the evils of drink and the following was the first of the many speeches and exhortations made by the founder of the movement:

'To the People of O'Connorville, 1847.
. . . Having placed you in that honourable and enjoyable situation let me now counsel you, and implore of you to attend to my advice. There is a beer shop adjoining your land; avoid it, I beseech you, as a PESTILENCE, for if any enemy can be the means of ousting you from the lovely spot on which it is my pride to locate you, it will be man's greatest, most vicious and inviting enemy—drunkenness.
I have earned a right to address you on this subject, because it is my boast to say that I have NEVER BEEN TIPSY in my life, and if I had been addicted to that base destroyer, I never should have had patience, never health, strength or constitution to have redeemed you from starving, and therefore I pray you to worship sobriety as the greatest and adorable friend and Deity.'

Meanwhile money continued to pour in, and when the times and the meagre wages of the type of people concerned are considered, the amount raised was indeed surprising, and not least to the originator of the scheme himself. Extracts from a further speech included:

'. . . This week's collection for this holy cause is nearly £3,200 (tremendous cheering) and mark what my greatest joy is—it is that the greatest portion of that had been snatched from the GIN PALACE and the BEER SHOP (cheers) so when the market for abstinence and virtue and industry was opened, those reviled for their drunkenness, their idleness and vice, soon took advantage of it. Yes! my friends, but let us have an inducement to be honest, sober and industrious, and I still pledge myself that if you meet a

The Plough, Rusper (Sussex)

New Inn, Gloucester (Glos)

Mermaid, Rye (Sussex)

Gate, Upper Braills (Warws)

Fleece, Birtsmorton (Worcs)

Star, Slad (Glos)

drunken man or even a woman in Manchester the creature is an object of envy, but woe to him who shall be branded as drunkard by the sober eyes of the watchful and prudent here. . .

Drunkenness is the first step to poverty, to crime and disgrace. You never see a teetotaller starving, or his family in misery.'

Unfortunately, O'Connor had quarrelled with most of the other Chartist leaders and now many of them began to make difficulties. The Poor Law Commissioners were called in to make an inspection and their report was that the settlers, mostly factory hands, would be unable to sustain themselves and would be eventually thrown on the poor rate. There must have been more than a modicum of truth in the assertion, for the men and women concerned were quite unused to agricultural tasks.

Within two years a select committee of the House of Commons was set up to enquire into the plan and months later found against the whole scheme, which was by then practically bankrupt. A Bill was brought before Parliament to wind up the affairs of the company and in 1851 a manager was placed in charge. A year later, poor O'Connor was pronounced insane and, when he died in 1855, the estate was auctioned at the *Swan*, Rickmansworth, (demolished about 1963). At the time of the closure, only three of the original settlers were still in possession of their plots.

Today, the four roads which were laid down still bear their original names, and one or two of the cottages are just as they were first built. They are all that remain of a dream which came true but failed miserably when put into practice.

It was a group of the miserable and disenchanted settlers who named the local inn the *Land of Liberty, Peace and Plenty*.

In South Shields (Co Durham) there is an inn which rejoices in the name of the *Balancing Eel*. Formerly called the *Grapes*, it is at the corner of Ocean Road and Woodbine Street and when it was purchased by Vaux Breweries in 1969, the new owners felt that it needed a new name which would be both unusual and have a nautical flavour, in view of its location. The search commenced and in 'Alice in Wonderland' they came across the verse:

You are old' said the youth 'one would hardly suppose
That your eye was as steady as ever;
Yet you balanced an eel on the end of your nose—
What made you so awfully clever?'

So the *Balancing Eel* it was, and the sign shows a mariner holding on to a rope and an eel balanced on his nose.

There are two theories about the name *Hawk & Buckle*, which is to be found in inns in many parts of the country. One is that it is derived from 'Falcon & Fetterlock', the falcon, of course, being the hawk and the fetterlock a shackle, or what could be a buckle from one of the badges of the House of York.

There is, however, a further, more likely theory. A buckle is not part of the equipment of falconry, but the art, or sport, has many terms of French as well as Arabic origin. It is likely, therefore, that the word buckle is a corruption of the French 'boucle' meaning buckle, swivel or staple. Another expression is 'en boucle', meaning imprisoned. When a hawk is not flying free, it is tethered to its perch or block by a long leash which terminates in a swivel. It seems very probable, therefore, that an imprisoned or tethered hawk would be termed a 'Hawk en Boucle' which, with an Englishman's tongue round it, could easily become *Hawk & Buckle*. Inns of this name include one at Llannefydd (Denbighshire).

The *Busby Stoop*, nr Thirsk (Yorks), was named after a macabre incident which took place near the present inn nearly 300 years ago. A Leeds clothier, Daniel Auty, had bought a house at Kirkby Wiske, nr Thirsk, which was known as Danotty Hall, and when he quickly became rich, rumour had it that he was an expert coiner. Later a man named Busby, who had married Auty's only daughter and become his partner, killed his father-in-law in the course of a quarrel, was arrested, found guilty and duly hanged. His body was hung in chains on a gibbet at the crossroads, and investigations revealed that Auty had indeed been a maker of counterfeit coins. The name of the inn presumably derived from a jeering reference to Busby swinging in chains.

Until a few years ago a chair which was said to have been Busby's stood in the bar of the inn and it was believed that anyone who sat in it would meet a tragic and early death. Several deaths are said to have followed instances of the legend being put to the test. Some years ago two RAF personnel from the nearby aerodrome sat in it as an act of bravado. When they left the inn that night to return to quarters, their car struck a tree and both were killed. In 1968, a group of building operatives working close by entered the inn for a lunchtime drink and a young labourer was persuaded to defy the superstition. He did so and within hours slipped off the roof of a house where he was working and was killed. It was at the request of the lad's father that the chair was removed from the bar and is now locked up in an outhouse.

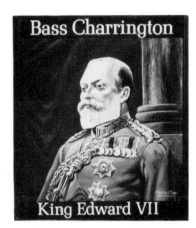

Top (*l to r*): *The Queen*, Penzance (Corn); *The Queen*, Upper Cwmbran (Mon); *The Queen*, Penzance (Corn)
Centre (*l to r*): *Kings Head*, Bledington (Glos); *King Edward VII*, Longlevens (Glos); *Kings Head*, Hursley (Hants)
Bottom (*l to r*): *Kings Head*, Wells (Som); *King Alfred*, Burrowbridge (Som); *King William*, Shepton Mallet (Som)

Nevertheless, Busby's ghost still seems to haunt the inn. Cups and saucers disappear from a cupboard in the kitchen, and other objects mysteriously move without human aid. Now a juke box occupies the place of the death chair in which, for a century or more, no 'local' would have sat for all the beer this fine old fifteenth-century inn could produce.

Danotty Hall Farm is still marked on the ordnance survey map.

Well-named is the *Mystery*, Portsmouth (Hants), for by some peculiar chance it remained undisturbed when the whole area of the harbour was re-developed. The *Mystery* still survives, tucked away between modern high buildings.

If ever there was a handsome and intriguing name for an inn it is *Ye Olde Tippling Philosopher*, Caldicot (Mon). Many theories have been advanced as to how it came to be so named, the most generally accepted being that it was once owned by a man called Tippling, a name still current in the district. Other stories endeavour to tie it up with a philosopher monk, but all fall down when it is recalled that there was formerly a *Tippling Philosopher* in aptly-named Liquor Pond Street, off Grays Inn Road, London. So we must assume that the tippling part at any rate comes from a dictionary definition 'Tippling-house —a house in which liquors are sold in small quantities—a public house.'

The Caldicot inn was a farmhouse some 400 years ago and the Philosopher's lounge has a stone to prove it. A massive one, it originally served as a lintel across the entrance to the great barn.

Well-sited is the *Gravediggers* inn, situated near the main gate of Highland Road cemetery, Portsmouth (Hants).

Colchester (Essex) is rightly proud of its history, and is to be congratulated on having perpetuated facets of it in the names of its inns.

Colchester was a strategic Roman settlement 2,000 years ago, and of sufficient importance for Queen Boadicea to attack it with her army and massacre the Roman occupants. Parts of the wall which encircled the town still remain and on top of the Balkerne Gate today stands the *Hole in the Wall*, which was previously known less appropriately as the *King's Head*.

Also in Colchester is the *King Coel*, which recalls the fact that Coel, the hero of the town, is identified with Cunobelin, the Iron Age king who reigned in the area in the first century AD. Coel was traditionally the father of Saint Helena, the mother of Constantine the Great. The nursery rhyme 'Old King Cole' can only be traced back to the seventeenth century, but Colchester's King Coel is documented over many centuries in the borough records.

Another Colchester inn, the *Silver Oyster* recalls a famous local industry and refers to the silver oyster gauges of the borough regalia. Their original purpose was to serve as the measure of the minimum size of oyster which it was permissable to harvest. The inn sign depicts an oyster and the fishing smack CK231, which is still on Essex waters and the oldest working boat of its kind in the country.

In the Colchester museum there are several old inn signs, including that of the *Three Cups* (now closed) and the seventeenth-century sign of the *King's Head*.

On a new housing estate in the area is the *Ancient Briton*, appropriately on Iceni Way.

The *Star of India*, Nunhead, London, has as its sign a replica of the medallion of that British order of chivalry known as 'The most Exalted Order of the Star of India'. Instituted by Queen Victoria in 1861, as a reward for services in and for India, the motto of the Order is 'Heaven's Light our Guide'.

In the reign of Henry III, about AD 1252, a charter was granted to a Corporation of the Lords Bailiff and Jurats of Romney Marsh (Kent). By the charter, twenty-four Lords were entrusted with the maintenance of flood protection and preventive works on Romney Marsh. The body was the first to undertake such work in the country and indeed, the first sea wall was built by them. Their duties continued through the centuries until the passing of the Land Drainage Act in 1930, when they were taken over by the newly-formed catchment boards. Unfortunately, about 1571 the hall and offices, together with all the corporation's records, were destroyed by fire. The hall was rebuilt in 1576.

Today the corporation, known as Romney Marsh Level, are the nominal freeholders of the present building, which is let as offices to the Kent River Authority and the Internal Drainage Boards on Romney Marsh. Tradition, however, lives on for at an annual meeting known as the Grand Lath, the bailiffs' sergeant is still appointed. Resplendent in his uniform, he is pictured on the sign of the *Bailiffs' Sergeant*, an inn at Jefferstone Lane, St Mary's Bay (Kent).

When Mr J. M. Duncan, a commissioned gunner in the Royal Navy, retired and took over the inn at Merstham (Surrey) in 1966, he set out to find an appropriate name for it. Learning that the land on which it stood belonged to the Jolliffe family, he enquired whether by any chance the family had naval connections. To his surprise, he found that Lt George Jolliffe of Merstham had served on HMS 'Bellerophon' at the battle of the Nile on 1 August 1798. The twenty-year-old lieutenant, who was killed in the action, was the son of William Jolliffe, MP for Petersfield 1766–1802, and there are tablets to both father and son in the local church. So the inn now proudly bears the name of *Jolliffe Arms* and the sign shows the family arms on one side and a scene from the naval engagement on the other.

Painted by Mr W. Pierce, Bass Charrington artist, the sign was unveiled by Cdr A. Hardy, RN, who at the time commanded HMS 'Victory', Nelson's ship at Portsmouth. Many of the present licensee's own trophies and mementoes of his thirty years' service in the Navy now adorn the bar.

The 'Bellerophon's' chief opponent in the battle of the Nile was the French flagship 'L'Orient', commanded by Admiral Casabianca. He had on board with him his ten-year-old son who refused to leave his father when the ship caught fire, and both were blown up with the ship. Only seventy were saved from a crew of hundreds. This inspired the poem 'Casabianca'—'The boy stood on the burning deck'—though the poet took some licence with the facts.

Nelson's captain, Benjamin Hallowell, presented him with a coffin he had had made for him from one of 'L'Orient's' timbers. Nelson was delighted and often went to inspect it at the undertaker's in Brewer Street, London, where he stored it. He was eventually buried in it.

Near Chichester (Sussex) is the *Selsey Tram*, which commemorates the tramway which ran from the outskirts of Chichester to Selsey for many years until it was lifted in 1932.

One of the most ancient inns in the British Isles is the famous *George*, Stamford (Lincs). The original building was owned by the Abbots of Croyland and, as such, must have been erected in AD 922. Later the abbey lands in the area passed to the Abbey of Peterborough. In the fifteenth century a new building arose on the site, though the medieval remains of the former building, including the crypt and a winding subterranean passage, are still to be found under what is today the cocktail bar.

Stamford has featured prominently in English history but easily the most exciting period for the *George* must have been when forty coaches a day passed through the town, pausing at the inn to change horses and refresh travellers. The two rooms just inside the front door of the present inn are a reminder of the activity which must then have prevailed. To the left is the door marked 'London', which opens onto a lounge richly panelled from floor to ceiling. This would have been where the southbound travellers waited for the London coach. Opposite, the York room served a similar purpose for northbound travellers.

In 1815, when the tenancy of the inn was advertised for sale, it had ten sitting-rooms, thirty-eight bedrooms and spacious outhouses. There was stabling for eighty-six horses, and the inn itself owned seventeen pairs of horses which were in constant demand.

If the coaching era caused activity, excitement was provided 100 years before when the eighth Earl of Exeter built Stamford's famous cockpit, with seats for 600 people. On race days in particular, matches were arranged until this form of entertainment was forbidden by law.

The *George* was famous wherever inns were discussed for many reasons. It was a meeting-place for sportsmen of all kinds who were always ready to take or place a wager. On one of these occasions a well-known local man undertook to ride the ninety miles from Piccadilly to the *George* within five hours. He left London at 8.0am and reached the *George* at 12.25, having made no less than thirteen changes of horse.

In its heyday the *George* received many famous and illustrious visitors, among them Charles I, William III and in 1768 the King of Denmark. In 1745, the Duke of Cumberland, son of George II, broke his journey there when returning victorious from Culloden. It was also a favourite haunt of Sir Walter Scott.

Tragedy, too, has visited the *George*. In 1714 as the tapster, following the Jacobite custom, drank kneeling on bare knees to the memory of Queen Anne, he was pierced to the heart with a sabre by one of the dragoons stationed in the town.

In latter years it has become a symbol of the old days by reason of its magnificent 'gallows' sign, one of the few remaining in the country. These signs were large structures which were suspended across the width of the thoroughfare and the main beam carried the name or sign of the inn.

Daniel Lambert, the most corpulent Englishman ever known, was a Leicestershire man and when the whole $52\frac{3}{4}$ stone of him went on a tour he visited the *George*. He died in the town in 1809, of fatty degeneration of the heart. His coffin was built on two axle trees and four wheels, and on it his body was taken to the burial ground of St Martins, Stamford Baron. A link remains at the *George*, where his walking stick is still to be seen.

If visitors to Britain wish to savour something of the Dickens era, then the *George*, Stamford, is a 'must'. Here is an ancient building, a great sign, a place where an English king (Charles I) visited, and last but by no means least, a giant mulberry tree, certainly 300 years old, which still gives up its luscious fruit for the benefit of those who call at the famous inn, as they have done for certainly nearly 500 years and probably some centuries before that.

Today but a tiny village, Lydford, on the western edge of Dartmoor (Devon), was in Saxon times a walled town built by Alfred during his campaigns against the Danes. A mint was established and later a castle was built where offenders against the stannary and forest laws were incarcerated. As late as 1512 it was described as 'one of the most heinous, contagious and detestable places in the realm'. After the twelfth century, Lydford deteriorated rapidly but in the sixteenth century the *Dartmoor* inn was already established and must have served not only the packhorse travellers across the moor but also, by virtue of its proximity to Plymouth, Drake, Raleigh and other Elizabethan captains. Certainly the long, squat building, with its low ceilings and winding corridors, massive fireplaces and contemporary atmosphere, can look back on a long history.

The *Sloop*, Scaynes Hill (Sussex) dates back to the middle of the last century, when the London, Brighton & South Coast Railway was being built. At that time the river Ouse was navigable up to the site and all the bricks and other material for building the viaduct on the main Brighton line between Balcome and Hayward's Heath were brought up the river in sloops and then transferred to small barges. The river is no longer navigable up to the *Sloop*, which now serves as the headquarters of the the local angling association.

It is fitting that in Oxford there should be an inn to serve as a reminder that in this city one of the truly great motorcars of the twentieth century was designed and manufactured over a period of fourteen years.

The first Bullnose Morris was made in April 1913, the initial model having a 1,018cc White & Poppe engine of 9hp. Officially known as the

Morris Oxford, it at once became immensely popular as an inexpensive family motor car and altogether 155,244 were built. It was followed by the 11.9hp Morris Cowley, which made its appearance during the first world war and was manufactured in considerable quantities after 1918. This was followed by the larger model Oxford with a 13.9hp engine.

History is told on this sign at Oxford

The *Bullnose Morris* was officially opened in March 1967, forty years after the car had ceased to be manufactured. The opening was quite an occasion, with the Lord Mayor of Oxford and many other notables in attendance. The interior of the inn has cars embossed on the walls, sectioned models of engines and other items connected with the car. The sign shows the car as in a draughtsman's drawing.

There is also a Bullnose Morris club, of which Lord Nuffield (formerly William Richard Morris and the founder of the firm) was the first president, a position he held until his death in 1963. He was followed by Mr K. C. Revis, MBE, who still holds the office. In 1968, Mr Revis took part in the eighth International Veteran & Vintage Car rally, and was driven by a friend from Cape Town to Durban, South Africa, in a 1926 Bullnose Morris Cowley —one of the first of the famous breed.

'The *Old Cock* inn 1712, licensed in the tenth year of Queen Anne' is the legend inscribed over the door of one of the oldest inns in Droitwich (Worcs). There are several quaint features about the place, not least the carvings which adorn the front of the building. Over the main door is one of a man with a frog coming out of his mouth, which is locally held to be a caricature of the infamous Judge Jeffreys. Also in the front wall of the inn is a medieval four-light window dated about 1320, which came from the old church of St Nicholas. The first church, built in Norman times, was destroyed by fire in 1290, and its replacement was taken over by the Roundheads in the Civil War, who used it as a barracks for the garrison. After this indignity, the church gradually became a ruin and the window found its way to the inn.

At Bath (Som) is the *Curfew* inn, with a descriptive sign which shows a village square with the curfew bell ringing in the church tower while Roundheads hurriedly shepherd the villagers into their homes. One worthy man has had his steeple-crowned hat knocked off his head in the melée.

An inn at Bishops Waltham (Hants) was for generations the *Wheatsheaf*, but after the relief on 18 May 1900 of Mafeking, which had been besieged by the Boers for seven months, the inn was renamed the *Mafeking Hero* in honour of the men of the village who had survived the siege.

For 110 years the *Cupid* inn served the people of Grove-hill and Cupid Green, Hemel Hempstead (Herts). It was a firm favourite, so that when in 1970, it was scheduled for demolition because of roadworks, a new *Cupid* was built in its place.

In the old days when pubs were on the roadside, one sign was all that was needed. But now that pubs are in open, landscaped areas there is more scope, and so when it came to designing a sign for the new pub, the architect decided to do something different and have a set of three signs with a story behind each. The signs were painted by Mr D. A. Clark of Watford and the first shows a cupid frowning at a young couple who have fallen out after an argument. In the second sign, the cupid has a mischievous look on his face as he fires his arrows at the hearts of the couple and finds his target. The third sign shows the couple in loving embrace—reunited as cupid hovers above them with a wink, a smile and a thumbs-up gesture.

So often it is courting contradiction to claim that an inn is the only one of that name, but there can surely be no question about the *20 Church-wardens*, Cockley Cley, Swaffham (Norfolk). One

imagines, too, that it would be difficult to find any inn where twenty churchwardens had their own tankard at the 'local', each engraved with the name of its owner and the parish he served.

The inn is a comparatively new one, having been opened in 1968, and received its name because it is in the centre of ten parishes of a a church group, each with two churchwardens. The parishes, which have a total population of 1,800 and are spread over an area of forty square miles, work as a group. All the churches are of ancient foundation and each parish was, or in some cases still is, the centre of a large estate. One of the parishes, Hilborough, had a long connection with the Nelson family, Lord Nelson's father, grandfather and other relations having, in turn, been rectors there throughout the eighteenth century. The great Admiral himself showed his affection for the village by adopting the title of Baron Nelson of the Nile and Hilborough.

The neighbouring parish of Bodney gave sanctuary to some Roman Catholic nuns who fled from the French Revolution and started a girls' school at Bodney which subsequently gained a fine reputation. Sixteen of these nuns, including a daughter of the Prince of Condé, lie buried in the churchyard.

In Queen Victoria Street, London, the *Black Friar* stands on a site occupied in medieval times by a monastery of the Dominican order. Monks are depicted on a copper panel fixed to the wall of the inn. The Dominicans came to London in the thirteenth century and set up a priory where Lincolns Inn now stands. Later they moved to Printing House Square, as it is known today. The district of Blackfriars owes its name to this establishment and it is interesting to recall that one of the bastions of Blackfriars bridge was designed like a pulpit to mark the association with the monks. It is quite obvious when travelling upstream.

In the west central district of London is the *Monks Tavern,* another associated with the Black Friars.

In Somerset, particularly in the area round Bristol and Bath, there are several inns named the *Blue Bowl*. A blue bowl was traditionally associated with punch, the ingredients of which were spirits, sugar, tea, lemon and water. The bowls were a speciality of the manufacturers of Bristolware. The sign at the *Blue Bowl*, Polsham (Som), is splendidly descriptive, showing a Bristolware bowl bearing the arms of the Vinters' Company and a list of the ingredients that made the drink. (Picture, p39.)

In the chancel of Shrivenham church (Berks), there is a monument over the grave of Admiral Samuel Barrington (1729–1800), and in the village there is the *Barrington Arms*. The Barrington family were long associated with Shrivenham and there is a monument in the village commemorating William Wildman Barrington, second Viscount and one-time Chancellor of the Exchequer.

At the *Bear,* in the market place of Devizes (Wilts), Sir Thomas Lawrence, the great portrait painter, spent his early years, for his father was the innkeeper. At that time the *Bear* was a favourite stopping-place for the gentry on their way to Bath and the precocious talents of the young Lawrence frequently provided entertainment for the guests. As well as demonstrating his artistic ability, the boy would also stand on the table to recite lines from Pope, Collins and Milton. Nevertheless, the inn did not prove very successful and when the boy was ten years old, the family moved to Bath. Later the youngster had a studio where he subsequently built up an immense practice as a popular artist. When he died in 1830 he was buried in St Paul's Cathedral.

Most old inns are steeped in history and tradition, and with some of them go, for good measure, a whole lot of superstitions. This is particularly so of *Ye Olde Cross* inn, Alnwick (Northumberland), which locally rejoices in the name of 'Dirty Bottles'. The reason is that the small bay window in the front of the inn contains seventeen wine bottles and casks covered by an accumulation of dust and cobwebs which has remained undisturbed for 150 years. The story goes that the owner was arranging them for display when he collapsed and died, and the legend grew that anyone touching them would suffer the same fate—so untouched they have remained. The name comes from an ancient stone cross, mounted on a shield said to have been stolen from Alnwick Abbey, which is built into the front of the inn. The cross is reputed to have been built into the wall at night, which may account for the fact that the shield is upside down.

It is rare to find political battles perpetuated in the name of an inn, but at Hilsea, nr Portsmouth (Hants), there is a sign in the form of a tiled panel which commemorates one of over sixty years ago. The inn, the *Coach & Horses,* was once owned by the War Office and had pre-viously been let to the Portsmouth & Brighton United Breweries at a rental of £125 per annum, but in July 1907 the War Office offered to sell it to the brewery company for £10,000. The deal was duly completed and the following year the Liberal government of Campbell-Bannerman, which included a number of teetotal reformers, put forward a Bill providing that public-house licences should endure only long enough to ensure a return of capital, and then the properties should subsequently be sold to the Government in return for compensation.

Naturally tempers on both sides flared up, particularly in Portsmouth where the sale of the inn was regarded as a flagrant instance of sharp practice, since it was felt that the government must have known about the proposed Act at that time.

On the one hand the brewers protested loudly against 'Socialism under the cloak of temperance,' whilst their opponents took an opposite view with equal fanaticism. John Burns, the doughty Labour orator, said: —

'Publicans do not like tramways; they carry people past the public-houses. They do not like the comfortable housing of the people; it counteracts their own attractions.

What the trade really does like, want and believe in is the warehousing of the women and children—with the workhouse in ultimate view for the public-house victims.'

In the event the Bill failed. A contemporary cartoon by Harry Furness, famous as a 'Punch' artist and caricaturist, showed a highwayman in the person of the then Chancellor of the Exchequer, Mr H. H. Asquith, and a coach owner, representing the licensed trade; being threatened by the pistol of the licensing Bill in Asquith's hand. The caption to the cartoon read: —

Asquith Highwayman—
'Stand and Deliver!'
Coach Owner.—
'But I have just paid your pal Haldane £10,000 for this lot.'
Highwayman.—'Clever Haldane! He knew I was coming along. You may keep the coach, but hand over the horses.'

The old *Coach & Horses* was pulled down about 1928 but fortunately the tiled reproduction of the cartoon was built into the wall of its successor, which was opened in 1931.

An unusual but attractive sign is that of the *Flying Scud*, Haggerston, London. It shows a topsail schooner running before the wind, a move-

Top (*l* to *r*): *The George*, Abbotsleigh (Som); *The Crown*, Minchinhampton (Glos); *Kings Arms*, Crewkerne (Som)
Centre (*l* to *r*): *Britannia*, Truro (Corn); *Kings Arms*, Cheltenham (Glos); *Crown*, Ibberton (Dorset)
Bottom (*l* to *r*): *Fleur de Lys*, Yeovil (Som); *Woolpack*, Weston-super-Mare (Som); *Rose & Crown*, Croscombe (Som)

21

ment known to old-time seamen as 'scudding' and carried out, according to the strength of the gale, either with a square sail on the foremast or running under bare poles. A once popular name in various forms for sailing-ships, 'scud' is quaintly defined in a marine dictionary of 1780 as 'a name given by seamen to the lowest and lightest clouds, which are most swiftly wafted along the atmosphere by the winds'. Situated in Hackney Road, E2, the inn is not far from the dock area and is much frequented by seamen.

There is another *Flying Scud,* also near the docks, at Plaistow.

The *Bear,* Woodstock (Oxon), is one of the original coaching inns of old England. It had already been dispensing hospitality for over 500 years when, in 1704, Queen Anne bestowed the royal manor of Woodstock on the Duke of Marlborough as a token of the country's gratitude for his victories over the French. Here Vanbrugh built the magnificent Blenheim Palace for the duke and his duchess, and 'Capability' Brown created the beautiful park with its great lake.

Woodstock has been a royal manor since time immemorial, the earliest records going back to fifty years before the Norman conquest, when Ethelred held a council there. Successive monarchs used the manor house as a lodge, from which they and their retinues hunted deer and wild boar in the forests which surrounded the place. Edward, the Black Prince, was born at Woodstock.

About the same time as the fine old church was built, the *Bear,* close by, opened for business and has been serving travellers ever since.

Almost opposite is the *Star,* whose sign shows the three wise men from the east on camels being guided to Bethlehem by the star.

Several inns are still owned by ecclesiastical authorities, but few, if any, can be older or their history more fully documented than the *Half Moon,* Stamford (Lincs), an ancient town full of interest. The inn has been the property of St George's Church since 1338, when the deeds were transferred by a local landowner, Walter of Skylyngton. The rent received for the inn is devoted to charitable purposes in the parish.

This ancient hostelry was reconstructed in 1938, and in the process an Early English arch, *circa* 1250, was discovered. It was undisturbed and still forms part of the building, though unfortunately it is now hidden.

Two other inns, now converted into private houses, were also once owned by St George's, a fine old church which has some beautiful glass and a record of the names of the illustrious members of the Order of the Garter since 1225.

In bygone centuries, signs with a religious affiliation were numerous but there are comparatively few left today. One of the few survivors is that of the *Coverdale,* Paignton (Devon), a reminder that Miles Coverdale (1488–1568) did some work on his English translation of the Bible nearby. This remarkable Yorkshireman became an Augustinian friar but left the order because of his belief in the Reformation movement. He produced his English version of the Bible, on which he had worked for sixteen years, in 1535. A friend of Sir Thomas More and Thomas Cromwell, he became Bishop of Exeter in 1551. The sign at Paignton shows Coverdale with the chained Bible and a bishop's mitre.

In the west central district of London is the *Gilbert & Sullivan,* commemorating the famous combination of Sir William S. Gilbert (1836–1911) and Sir Arthur Sullivan (1821–91), who produced many delightful and amusing operas. Sullivan was the composer and Gilbert wrote the lyrics. Their first joint effort was produced at the Gaiety Theatre, London, in 1871. Though there was constant friction between them, their partnership was highly successful and their comic operas became famous throughout the civilised world.

In the eighteenth century a fishing fleet owned by a local family named Hewitt was based at Barking (Essex). The fleet was known as the Short Blue Line and in recent years a new inn erected on a housing estate in the vicinity has been named *Short Blue*—yet another example of an inn's sign perpetuating local history. Barges still use the town quay as they have done for generations, and another inn is named *Barge Aground,* a reminder that not all of them caught the tide.

The village of Wedmore (Som) has seen several episodes of English history at close range. It was here that King Alfred signed his peace treaty with the Danes in AD 878. Some 800 years later the battle of Sedgmore was fought in the dykes nearby. The area is famous for its willows and in World War II the local craftsmen concentrated their output on panniers which, packed with arms and other necessities of war, were dropped over enemy territory to aid the underground resistance movement.

How long the 'local', the *George*, has been there is not definitely known, but certainly it was a coaching inn in the fourteenth century. Its courtyard, dovecote and entrance all help to make a perfect picture, but the real atmosphere is to be found in the cellar bar where mementoes and curiosities adorn the walls, There is, too, a bale of hay but that is neither an oversight nor a curiosity, as it is the best of all smoke extractors.

The inn's sign is an equestrian portrait of King George I. The artist, Stanley Chew, tired of the usual hackneyed portraits, wanted something different and he certainly achieved it, for the sign is both attractive and distinctive.

In the same area is the *King Alfred,* Burrowbridge, Alfred hid close by while waiting the outcome of negotiations which brought the Danes to submission. A ring bearing the words 'Alfred had me made' was found nearby and now forms the motif of the inn sign. (Picture, p15.)

The *Red Lion*, Wingham (Kent), was once the property of an order of monks, but was confiscated on the dissolution of the monasteries in the reign of Henry VIII. Parts of the building date back to 1286.

Inns named after the hero of Waterloo, the Duke of Wellington, are numerous. Probably unique, however, is the situation of the *Hero of Waterloo*, a few miles north of Portsmouth (Hants) in the small town known as Waterlooville, so named because many of the victorious troops rested at the hamlet which was en route to their barracks after landing at Portsmouth. The present inn is comparatively new and stands on the site of its predecessor, which was said to be haunted. Waterlooville, incidentally, is only one of twenty villages or hamlets in the British Isles bearing the name Waterloo.

Hereward the Wake, the Lincolnshire squire who, so legend tells us, held the isle of Ely against William the Conquerer in 1070, has lent the second half of his name to the *Wake*, nr Epping (Essex). The Wake family are said to have been landowners in the district.

One of the strangest names for an inn must surely be that of the *Bunch of Carrots*, at the hamlet of Hampton Bishop, in Herefordshire. The name does not refer to the vegetable, but is believed to derive from a rock formation in the River Wye, beside which the inn stands. The place has an ancient history but the earliest conveyance of the property to have been found by Welcome Inns Ltd, who now own it, is dated 1854, in which year it changed hands for £400!

In Nelson (Lancs) there is an *Hour Glass* and in each bar there is indeed an hour glass. It was the practice in seventeenth-century churches to have hour glasses attached to the pulpit, or in easy view of the preacher, so that he could time his sermon. One glass in All Saints church, Newcastle on Tyne (Northumberland) was arranged to run for $1\frac{1}{2}$ hours, but even so it sometimes had to be turned before the sermon was completed.

Now the inn at Nelson can surely claim a unique distinction in using an hour glass to run out the sands for closing time.

There is another *Hour Glass* at Exeter (Devon).

The *Henry Fielding*, Dunball, nr Bridgwater (Som), has a fine sign showing the eighteenth-century novelist and playwright in profile. Born near Glastonbury in 1707, Fielding was the son of an army officer. He began writing plays, comedies and farces before he was thirty and his first work was produced at Drury Lane in 1728. Difficulties over the licensing of plays, and officialdom's attitude to the stage and players, made him turn to the legal profession and he was called to the Bar in 1740. His best known work, that great novel 'Tom Jones', was written in 1749 and enjoyed a tremendous success. He died in 1754 in Lisbon, to which he had taken his wife and family on a voyage, and was buried there in the English cemetery. Only one authentic portrait of him is known to exist, a pen-and-ink drawing believed to be by Hogarth, and the sign at Dunball has undoubtedly been based upon it.

The Cornish family of Killigrew is famous for its many members who have served their country, and the *Killigrew Arms*, Falmouth (Cornwall), reminds us of them. It was Sir Robert Killigrew (1579–1633) who probably did most for the Duchy. He visited Sir Walter Raleigh in the Tower, was knighted by James I, was keeper of Pendennis Castle and, in 1625, won a grant from the king to repair the strongholds of St Mawes, St Michael's Mount and Pendennis Castle. The sign of the Falmouth inn displays the Killigrew coat of arms.

When a new inn was built at Rickmansworth (Herts) a few years ago, it was intended to name it *William Penn* after the Quaker who was so persecuted that he left England for America, where, in 1682, he founded Pennsylvania. But when it was pointed out that Penn was not only a very pious man but also a life-long teetotaller, it was decided to call it the *Keystone* instead.

On Southsea Common (Hants) is the *Wheelbarrow*, supposedly named after the transport used by the landlord of the inn to return to his quarters the captain of nearby Southsea Castle, who habitually dined and wined only too well at the inn. History does not record whether the captain had to call on this conveyance when, during the Civil War, Cromwell's troops captured the castle without a shot being fired.

It is sometimes said that the *Old Mint* inn, Southam (Warks), was so named because it occupies the building where coins were once minted. Many towns had this right until the practice was ended in the reign of Edward VI, but there is no evidence that Southam ever enjoyed the privilege and it is more than likely that the name came from a sweet—the mint. In the Restoration period of the seventeenth century, sweet mint shops, where they were made and sold, were very popular.

The *Picton*, Newport (Mon), remembers that fine soldier of the Napoleonic Wars, Sir Thomas Picton (1758–1815). A Pembrokeshire man, he had a brilliant career in the campaigns in Portugal and Spain, but later achieved even greater fame. He conducted the siege of Badajoz and led the assault, in which he was wounded. At Waterloo, the final battle of the Napoleonic Wars, he was killed by a musket ball when leading a charge. His body was taken to England and rested one night at the *Fountains* inn, Canterbury (Kent), a famous and very ancient inn which was destroyed by enemy action in World War II.

Music has been associated with English inns throughout the centuries. The music-hall had its beginning in an inn and earlier still, in 1790, the composition which was to become the American national anthem was first played in a London tavern.

Organs, however, are comparative rarities in an inn, so that the Compton organ in the *Plough*, Great Munden (Herts) [population about 400] gives this country inn a special claim to fame. Moreover, the instrument is so large that the inn had to be partially rebuilt to accommodate it.

The story began in 1937, when a superb and mighty organ was installed in the newly-built 2,600-seat Gaumont Cinema at Finchley in North London. It was played by many great theatre organists until 1966, when it was made redundant. Hearing of this, Gerald Carrington, mine host of the *Plough*, set off in haste to purchase the instrument, giving no thought as to how he would accommodate it. A keen organist, he had served an apprenticeship as a 'senior voicer' and 'tonal finisher', and had later held a senior position with the John Compton Co, a famous firm of organ makers who had also built the Gaumont organ.

With the help of his brother, he dismantled the instrument in London and brought it down to the *Plough*. His first thought had been to install it in a barn at the back of the inn and keep it for private use, but his brother, a vintage-car enthusiast, already had the place littered with car bodies, engines and the like. Then Gerald had an inspiration. Why not build a new lounge bar to house his 'baby' and have public performances which his customers could enjoy? It took a long time to obtain planning permission, architect's designs and the like, and meanwhile the work of complete overhaul and restoration proceeded.

Eventually, in December 1967, the new lounge was built, the organ installed, the services of guest artists obtained and there was a grand opening night.

The organ comprises some 900 pipes, and is a remarkably fine piece of craftsmanship. Its wide range of effects includes drums, cymbals and xylophones, and there are 200 automatic and finger-operated stops, key tabs and pistons, Altogether an assembly of the most intricate playing and sound control units ever devised as a single instrument.

Nowadays it is common to see the new lounge crowded and an overspill of latecomers in the narrow road outside listening to the only true pipe organ of its size and kind to be heard in any inn throughout the world. Not only the 'locals' come, but many visitors from nearby towns and villages as well.

A 'slice' of tradition is associated with the *Sirloin*, Hoghton, a few miles from Blackburn (Lancs), for close by is Hoghton Tower where, in 1617, a visiting king, James I, created the term 'sirloin' when he knighted a loin of beef. The king is said to have performed the ceremony when visiting Sir Richard Hoghton, the first Baronet. This interesting piece of history was recalled in a High Court action in 1969, when the oak table on which the king 'knighted' the beef was saved from the saleroom. For centuries the table has been owned by the De Hoghton family, and the trustees of the estate, who brought the action, obtained a temporary court order preventing the table from being moved and sold with other antiques.

Voted the best of the 300 inn signs entered in the Festival of Britain exhibition in 1951 was that of the *Roundstone,* East Preston (Sussex). The sign was based on an ancient legend about a suicide who was buried at the crossroads. The parish authorities, taking no chances, placed a massive millstone over the grave and drove a stake through the hole in the centre to prevent the spirit of the poor wretch haunting the neighbourhood. The sign makes the story quite clear, even to the skeleton's grimace at the weight of the stone. It was the custom in earlier days to inter suicides and witches at the parish boundaries, as no one wished to have them buried within their parish.

Rare, curious and in the wrong place is a large memorial tombstone standing outside the *Sun* inn, Bilsdale, a few miles north of Helmsley (Yorks). It commemorates Bobbie Dawson, whipper-in for some sixty years to the Bilsdale Hunt, one of the oldest in the country. When he died in 1902 at the ripe old age of eighty-six, local folk subscribed for a stone to be erected over his grave. The parson, however, objected as the carving on the stone portrayed a fox's mask, brush and a whip. So a plain stone was erected over the grave in the Chop Gate churchyard, and the 'locals' installed the original memorial outside the *Sun* inn, from which so often the old huntsman had set out. At the old man's funeral his favourite brown hunter, his spurs, cap and the Bilsdale hunting horn followed the funeral cortège. The present inn was erected in 1913, replacing a very ancient one, and has always been known locally as 'the Spout' because drinking water used to come from a spout in a field nearby.

An attractive historical sign, Bideford (Devon)

The sign at the *Sun*, Bruton (Som) is of mythological origin, for it represents a brooch associated with the dog-days of Roman times. These were days of great heat which the Romans knew as the six to eight hottest weeks of the summer. They assumed that the dog-star Sirius, rising with the sun, added to its heat, making this the warmest period of the year.

It is strange that there are not more signs to honour Sir Richard Grenville, the courageous Elizabethan sea-dog who, when in 1591 he met up with a greatly superior fleet of Spanish ships, decided to stand and fight it out. His ship the 'Revenge' (500 tons, 250 crew), fought for fifteen hours against terrific odds. Fifteen Spanish ships were beaten off, two were sunk, two disabled and 2,000 of the enemy killed or drowned, With hardly a man unscathed, Grenville's order to blow up his ship was not obeyed and he was carried aboard an enemy ship where he died of wounds two days later. A handsome sign commemorates the man and the battle at the *Sir Richard Grenville*, Bideford (Devon). (Picture, p25.)

The mundane name of the *New* inn, Ross-on-Wye (Herefordshire) was changed in 1969 to the *Eagle*, to commemorate the spaceflight of the three American astronauts, Collins, Aldrin and Armstrong. The sign shows Armstrong descending from the spacecraft 'Eagle' to become the first man to walk on the moon. A good instance of how inn signs keep pace with events. (Picture, p27.)

Furnished in eighteenth-century nautical style, the *Square Rigger*, near the Monument, London, has the appropriate atmosphere and fittings include decking, ship's rigging, lanterns, stuffed seagulls and even storm recordings.

Apollo, the god of Greek and Roman mythology, always represented in ·art as the perfection of youthful manhood, has been captured perfectly astride a white stallion, with the sun as a background, on the sign of the *Sun* inn, Yeovil (Som). Stanley Chew was the artist responsible for this attractive sign. (Picture, p27.)

At Peterborough (Northants) there is a *Paul Pry*, a legendary figure with no occupation of his own who was always interfering in other people's business. He is the principal character in a comedy by John Poole.

An attractive story is associated with the *Sexey's Arms*, Blackford, Wedmore (Som). It tells of Hugh Sexey, a poor boy of the sixteenth century who made his way in the world and won Elizabeth I's favour, eventually rising to become one of the seven auditors of the Exchequer. As a reward for his services, he was granted the manor of Blackford and, among other offices, was a governor of King's School, Bruton, in 1599. In his will he decreed that his lands should revert to his tenants in return for only a peppercorn rent, and the income should be used to run a school and a hospital. A trust carries on the arrangements to this day. The sign of the inn shows the benefactor as a boy, together with his coat of arms: a ship to represent trade and a castle to denote his royal favour.

The *Triple Plea*, nr Halesworth (Suffolk), has a sign depicting a man on his deathbed surrounded by a parson, a doctor and a lawyer, whilst in the background is the devil himself, complete with pitchfork. As usual, there are several theories as to its meaning, but the one generally accepted is that the three professionals are arguing as to who has the greatest claim to the body, while the devil bides his time, waiting for the appropriate moment to make his bid. Like the *Four Alls*, there are other variations of this picture on inn boards of the same name in other parts of the country, but the meaning is general.

Of the several inns named *World's End*, perhaps the best known is the one situated on the riverside at Knaresborough (Yorks). Its sign depicts a motorcoach falling with the town bridge into the river Nidd, which runs through a deep limestone gorge below. This stems from a prediction by the famous local soothsayer, Mother Shipton, who announced that when Knaresborough bridge falls for the third time it will be the end of the world.

Mother Shipton first appears in records in 1641, but is said to have been born Ursula Southiel nearly 200 years earlier. Over the centuries a mass of predictions attributed to her have been published, including 'Carriages without horses shall go' and 'Under water men shall walk, shall sleep and talk'. She was reputed to have predicted the end of the world in 1861 and thousands of country people gathered in churches that year to pray for deliverance. In 1873 a publisher confessed to having invented the predictions, but nonetheless, many people continue to quote and even believe in her alleged prophecies.

An altogether different illustration of the *World's End* is at Ecton (Northants), where the sign shows

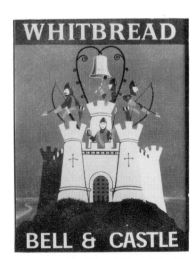

Top (*l to r*): *The Moon*, Wootton-under-Edge (Glos); *The George*, Bathampton (Som);
The Eagle, Ross-on-Wye (Herefs)
Centre (*l to r*): *The Sun*, Yeovil (Som); *Hooden Horse*, Wickhambreaux (Kent); *Mermaid*, Paignton (Devon)
Bottom (*l to r*): *Crystal Palace*, Bath (Som); *Bell & Castle*, Horsley (Glos); *Jack-in-the-Green*, Rockbeare (Devon)

the horse of a medieval traveller rearing up on its hind legs at the edge of a precipice.

Sir William Maynard Gomm (1784–1875), son of a soldier, had the distinction of being gazetted a lieutenant in the 9th Regiment before he was ten years of age, in recognition of his father's service. He had taken part in several campaigns before he was twenty, fought in all the major wars, campaigns and battles over a period of sixty years and eventually became Commander-in-Chief, India. This fine and popular soldier died at the age of ninety-one. The *Sir William Gomm*, Rotherhithe, London, SE16, commemorates him, as does a road of his name, and with such a record as his, it is only surprising that there are not more inns named after him.

Glencoe, Argyle (Scotland), has often been described as a dark glen of sorrow, because of the infamous massacre which took place there on 13 February 1692. The government had issued a proclamation in Scotland offering indemnity for past offences to all clan chiefs who, not later than 1 January 1692, would lay down their arms and take an oath of loyalty to William III. Alistair MacDonald of Glencoe, head of the clan MacDonald, was five days late in taking the oath, due largely to having been delayed by appalling weather. Five weeks later, soldiers under the command of Capt Robert Campbell of Glenlyon gained admittance to Glencoe under a subterfuge, and ruthlessly murdered the MacDonald of Glencoe and thirty-eight members of his clan.

Today, the *King's House* in Glencoe is believed to be Scotland's oldest inn. Its true age is not known, but certainly it was an inn before its use after the battle of Culloden in 1746 as a barracks for the troops of George III. They were stationed there to keep the Highlanders in subjection and to try and capture Bonnie Prince Charlie, the 'young Pretender' with a price of £30,000 on his head. The building was still being used as a military outpost in the reign of William IV (1830–37).

Glencoe, by reason of its history and magnificent scenery, today draws thousands of tourists and the *King's House*, now thoroughly modernised, is well equipped to offer them its hospitality.

At Peckham Rye, London, is the *Lord Lyndhurst*. This honours John Singleton Copley, who became Baron Lyndhurst in 1827. Born in Boston, Massachusetts, USA, in 1772, he came to England at an early age and studied law at Lincoln's Inn. His defence of one of the Luddite rioters in 1812 brought his brilliant talents into the public eye and

in 1824 he became Attorney General, a position he held three times. He died in 1863. There does not seem to be any obvious reason why he should have been honoured by an inn sign in Peckham Rye.

In and around Bath are several inns bearing the name *Bladud*, *Bladud Arms*, or *Bladud's Head*. These refer to the mythical king of England, who was father of King Lear. Legend says he built the city of Bath, studied magic and dedicated the city's springs to Minerva after he had been cured of leprosy by immersing himself in the waters. He did all this for Bath but alas, though his name is remembered, he does not figure on a sign.

At Seaford, nr Newhaven (Sussex), is the newly built *Buckle* inn. For centuries an inn named 'Buckle' stood on the site and when the new building was planned the brewers decided to rename it the 'Goldfish' as a tribute to the club of that name composed of RAF personnel rescued from 'ditched' aircraft during the war. The 'locals' refused to accept the new name and so *Buckle* it remains.

The original name is associated with the famous Sussex family of Pelham, who had a house near the village of Bishopstone which, having no inn of its own, was served by the *Buckle*. Sir John Pelham, who fought in the wars of Edward III in France, is said to have captured King John of France by seizing the buckle of his belt, probably at Poitiers in 1356. As a reward, he was allowed to incorporate the buckle in his coat of arms.

Sir John's son, John de Pelham, was in the service of John of Gaunt and later became Constable of Pevensey Castle and Treasurer of England under Henry IV.

Little wonder, with such illustrious patrons, that the Seaford people wished to retain the centuries-old name of their inn, the modern version of which is modelled on the Martello towers which were strategically placed to defend England against Napoleonic invasion.

At Watford (Herts) is the *Joseph Benskin* and quite a story lies behind the name. In the eighteenth century there were few private estates which did not have their own brewhouses from which to provide beer for the servants and farm labourers. From these beginnings it was but a step for one landowner to agree to supply the needs of his neighbours, and if one of the brews was especially popular, he might have gone farther and agreed to supply other licensed houses or licensees. In such a way trading breweries probably came into existence.

The foundation of the Cannon Brewery cannot be traced, but it was certainly in existence in 1750. The water of the river Thames had long been considered admirable for brewing but when, as the population and pollution increased, the water became heavily contaminated, the Thames-side breweries had to move their premises. The Cannon Brewery which moved to Watford (Herts) may be considered typical. Early in the nineteenth century it passed into the hands of the Dyson family, who ran the concern as a public brewery.

At about this time a lad of thirteen ran away from the village of Seagrave (Leics), where his father was vicar. The boy made his way to London, where he was friendless and destitute. He was Joseph Benskin, who soon became apprenticed to an apothecary and later the owner of the *Castle & Falcon* hotel in the city. Hard work and natural business ability made him prosper and he purchased control of 'Limmers', which is said to have been the first hotel in the modern sense in London.

In 1865 or thereabouts, Joseph Benskin retired to Turnham Green, but in 1867 he came to Watford, a town well known for its beautiful surroundings and healthy air, and bought the Cannon Brewery from the Dyson family. Joseph Benskin applied all his energy to the development of this venture and with his knowledge of the licensed trade, especially in London, very soon increased the weekly output of 100 barrels per week many times over. In later years, before his death in 1877, he was assisted in the business by his son, John Pusey.

Unfortunately, John suffered from ill health and early blindness, and on old Joseph's death the management of the brewery devolved upon his widow, assisted by John, and the managing brewer, Walter Green, who married Maria Benskin, old Joseph's daughter. It is of interest that at this period the three main breweries in Watford were controlled by Mrs Healey, Mrs Mary Ann Sedgwick and Mrs Joseph Benskin.

In 1885, James A. Panton came to Watford from Panton's Wareham Brewery, having been well trained as a brewer in new scientific methods. Just previous to this Joseph's third son, Thomas Benskin, who had been working as an architect in London, returned to Watford and the partnership of Thomas Benskin and James A. Panton continued to develop the Cannon Brewery under the name of Benskin & Co. Agencies were opened in many towns, including Eastbourne, Brighton, Southend, Aldershot and in several London stores, and within twenty-five years of old Mr Benskin coming to Watford the weekly output from the Cannon Brewery had increased more than twelve-fold. In 1898

the name of the company was changed to Benskin's Watford Brewery Ltd and the building of a new brewery was completed in the same year.

Thomas Benskin was well known in Watford with his square beard, frock coat and silk hat. He first came from town daily by train, then lived in the brewery house and finally at Glenthorn, more recently known as an RAF headquarters at Stanmore. He could be seen daily driving in his coach to meet his partner and late co-director, Mr Panton, at the brewery.

The *Joseph Benskin* inn at Watford is remarkably well documented, and was formerly known as the 'Compasses', probably because in 1725 it was bought as a going concern by Ralph Vaughn, a carpenter. His son succeeded him as owner, and when he sold the premises in 1740, mention was made of '5 large vessels in the cellar'. There was a brewhouse attached and the buildings were all adjacent to the market place.

Owner followed owner and when in 1798, it was kept by a Mary Timberlake, the building was a picturesque two-storey house of indeterminate age. When the inn was rebuilt in 1930, a fifteenth-century window from the old building was incorporated in the new one, and after further alterations in 1966 the house was renamed *Joseph Benskin*.

The Benskin Brewery is no longer an independent concern but is integrated with the Ind Coope group.

In the world of inn signs names are not by any means always what they seem, and this is particularly true of the *York Minster*, Dean Street, in London's Soho, and the only one of its name in Britain. No one knows with any certainty why it was so called, the most popular supposition being that, like so much of Soho, it was once Church property.

The story of the inn goes back some seventy years when a young man from the village of St Quentin came to London and became the first Frenchman ever to be granted a licence for a London public house. He was Victor Berlemont and he very soon introduced some of his native customs so that the pub became more like a Paris *bistro*, than a Cockney's 'local' and has for long been popularly known as the 'French House'.

A speciality of the house is wines by the glass and the shelves hold an arresting array of bottles containing pernod, byrrh, suze, cap corse and mandarin. But the *pièce de résistance* is a curious machine comprising a glass cistern fitted with a silver lid and a number of little taps which dominates the area behind the bar.

This is an 'absinthe carafe' and when a measure of the spirit has been poured into a glass, it is then placed under one of the taps. Water from the carafe drips slowly through a perforated spoon over a lump of sugar above the glass. The action of the sweetened water turns the absinthe cloudy, the whole process taking about five minutes.

The sale of absinthe, a distillation of a bitter plants known as wormwood, has been forbidden in France and other European countries since 1914, when excessive addiction to the 'tipple' was suspected by the French government of reducing the birthrate. True or not, the ban was later ratified by the League of Nations. The story goes that the British representative at Geneva did not know what absinthe was and so it can still be sold in Britain, though it is almost unobtainable.

Another fascinating feature of the *York Minster* is its picture gallery, which contains photographs of many international celebrities who, when in London, always considered a visit to the pub a 'must'. The great names include those of the boxing champion, George Carpentier, Maurice Chevalier, Mistinguette, Charlie Chaplin and a host of others.

During the last war, unknown to his customers who included men serving with the Free French forces, Victor Berlement took part in the regular BBC broadcasts to occupied France.

The founder's son, Gaston, who was born on the premises, served in the RAF during the war and now presides over this little bit of France in England bearing the name of a cathedral in a city 200 miles distant.

At Pickering (Yorks) is the *Lettered Board* inn and one story goes that it was granted a charter by George III. As in those days the inn was but a small alehouse and most unlikely to have been deemed worthy of a charter, a more probable theory is that the landlord came by a document, nothing of which he could read except perhaps 'George III'. It was, however, used as a copy for the signboard and for years the wording has been a source of query and speculation.

An inn has stood in High Street, Hastings (Sussex), for some hundreds of years, and what name it previously carried is not now known. The place was reconstructed in 1934 and in addition to uncovering beams 400 to 500 years old, the remains of what appeared to be a reredos was brought to light. This was handed over to the rector of the parish, who housed it in St Clement's church. The inn is now the *Jenny Lind*, named after the great soprano famed as the 'Swedish nightingale'. Her real name was Madam Goldschmidt and she died at Malvern (Worcs) in 1887.

There is another inn named *Jenny Lind* at Sutton (Surrey).

In Grays Inn Road, London, is the *Pindar of Wakefield*. A pindar was one who was in charge of the village pound and impounded straying cattle. George-a-Green was the mythical 'Pindar' of Wakefield who resisted Robin Hood, Will Scarlett and Little John when they attempted to commit a trespass in Wakefield. One who will do his duty, come what may, has come down in the language 'as good as George-a-Green'.

The first double-decker warship in the English Navy was a galleon built in 1514 and named after Henry VIII—'Henry Grace à Dieu'—though popularly known as the 'Great Harry'. At Hemel Hempstead (Herts) this is recalled by the *Great Harry*. The original of the three-masted vessel pictured on the sign was of about 1,500 tons, with an armament of 72 guns and a crew of 700. Launched at Woolwich, she was rebuilt at Portsmouth twenty-five years later, in 1539, and renamed 'Edward' in 1547. She was accidentally destroyed by fire in 1553.

At St Albans (Herts) is another *Great Harry* but the sign here depicts Henry himself.

Another famous old ship is commemorated by the *Royal George*, Worcester (Worcs), which carries an inspiring sign showing the vessel wearing the royal standard, indicating the presence of the monarch on board. A first-rate of completely new design, the 'Royal George', 2,047 tons and 178ft in length, was built at Woolwich Dockyard in 1756 and foundered off Spithead in 1782 when hurrying to the relief of Gibraltar. (Picture, p49.)

At Three Cocks, near Glasbury (Radnorshire), the inn is also the *Three Cocks*. It is hilly country and though three cock birds are illustrated on the sign, the inn really took its name from the three cock horses which were kept handy to be hitched on to freight waggons to help them over the gradients. The cock horse led the trace horse.

From this stemmed the children's game when 'reins' were fastened to the arms of the leader of the three. The last one in the file held the reins and the middle one was free. The pace was governed by the first or 'cock' horse. Hence, too, the reference in the nursery rhyme, 'Ride a cock horse to Banbury Cross'.

Top (l to r): *Castle Eden*, Durham; *Village Inn*, Twyning (Glos); *Castell Y Bwch*, Henllys (Mon)
Centre (l to r): *Post Office*, Stroud (Glos); *Elm Tree*, Radstock (Som); *Viaduct*, Monckton Combe (Som)
Bottom (l to r): *Hearts of Oak*, Drybrook (Glos); *Northgate*, Caerwent (Mon); *Goldfinger*, Highworth (Wilts)

STORIES OF INNS AND THEIR SIGNS

When the transition from coach transport to the railway was completed, many previously busy inns found themselves relegated to a relative backwater. Those that stayed in business found, after many years, that the wheel had turned full circle and with the advent of the motorcar their fortunes improved. In more recent times extensive new road works and the construction of motorways have repeated the pattern and inns which had enjoyed great popularity as roadhouses in the 1950s again became relegated to secondary roads. It is a pattern particularly evident where the main traffic stream is being diverted to by-pass towns, and one of the most interesting examples of this is the situation of the *Shepherd & Flock*, just outside Farnham (Surrey). The new section and roundabout of the A31 has turned the inn's premises into an island site around which traffic is constantly circulating.

Redevelopment in the centre of towns is also responsible for the loss of many ancient and sometimes historic inns. In 1969, the site on which the *Royal* had stood in the centre of Truro (Corn) for nearly 200 years, was sold to make way for a supermarket. The inn had been built as a coaching inn in 1789 at the cost of £2,000.

Close to Stansted airport at Tiy Green, near Stansted Mountfitchet (Essex), is an inn which, when modernised by the brewers, Rayment & Co, a year or so ago, was renamed the *Ash*. Reference to 'Brewer's Dictionary of Phrase and Fable' shows the origin of the sign to be the world tree which, with its roots and branches, binds together heaven, earth and hell. A fountain represents great virtues and in the tree, which drips honey, sit an eagle, a squirrel and four stags. The tree is a late addition to Scandinavian mythology and the name by which it is known, 'Yggdrasil', was probably that of one of the winds.

The year 1971 was chosen to launch an appeal fund for the Gurkhas, those fine fighting men from Nepal who have served with the British Army for over 150 years. It was then that Mr B. Shillaker, who had always admired the Gurkhas, decided to rename his inn, the *Gurkha*. Former regimental officers rallied round to obtain appropriate mementoes and today this inn at Iver (Bucks) has many items which recall much of the history of the force.

The first Gurkha regiment was raised in 1815 from prisoners-of-war taken during a punitive raid into Nepal by British troops. It was soon apparent what superb fighting men they were and eventually ten Gurkha regiments were formed, followed later by transport, signal, engineer and parachute detachments. Six regiments have now been transferred to the Indian Army.

The centrepiece of the decoration in the bar is a Victoria Cross bearing the names of the twenty-six Gurkhas who won this coveted award. The first was awarded during the Indian mutiny in 1858, and the last in Borneo in 1965.

On one wall of the bar is a mural depicting a typical Nepalese village scene, painted by Stephanie Mcgurk, the wife of a Gurkha officer. There is also a display of all the regimental badges, as well as one from HMS 'Gurkha'. Other items on display include a captured Japanese sword, maps of Nepal and pictures autographed by Field-Marshal Lord Harding and Brigadier Sir John Smyth VC, who served with the regiment.

The fine sign by artist G. E. Mackenney depicts on one side Subadar-Major Santabir Gurung who, on the death of Edward VII, became the first Indian Army soldier to stand guard over his sovereign at a lying-in-state. On the reverse is shown a typical subadar-major of the 1910 period.

Naturally the men from Nepal appreciate the tribute to them and already nearly 300 have called and signed the visitors' book at the *Gurkha*.

Of the hundreds of coaching inns that existed in the eighteenth and early nineteenth centuries there are now only a few which retain the courtyard where the coaches began and ended their journeys, and fewer still which have kept the balconies which gave on to the bedrooms for travellers.

One such, the *New* inn, Gloucester (Glos), was built in 1457, forty years before Columbus discovered the American mainland. The story of its building by Abbot Thokey to accommodate pilgrims is well known, but that this lucrative pilgrim traffic made it possible largely to rebuild Gloucester's magnificent cathedral is not so well known.

It was from the balcony of the *New* inn that the ill-fated nine-day queen, Lady Jane Grey, was proclaimed and presented to the citizens of Gloucester. In only two other places in the realm did this happen.

The inn today serves as a visual record of the building of the Middle Ages. It has venerable oak and chestnut beams, a stone-flagged courtyard and, above all, an atmosphere which has been carefully preserved despite the alterations and additions of recent years. Incorporated in the rebuilt wine press bar is a Tudor doorway which came from the old Gaiety theatre in London, and some fourteenth-century church windows.

The *Imperial Arms*, Chislehurst (Kent), was formerly the *Windmill* inn and as such was known to the exiled Emperor of France and his family when, after the debacle at Sedan in 1870, Napoleon III was captured by the Prussians. His wife, Eugenie, left France and resided at Chislehurst, where she was later joined by the fourteen-year-old Prince Imperial, and then by his father. The family settled down and were absorbed into the community.

The Emperor died after two years of exile, but the young prince entered Woolwich Military Academy and was later commissioned as an officer in the Royal Horse Artillery. He fought in the Zulu War and was killed in an ambush in 1879.

At Esher (Surrey) there is the *Orleans Arms* where, until a few years ago, a pair of the Emperor's boots was on display in a glass case. Outside this inn is a rare eighteenth-century milestone giving distances to places in the vicinity. In coaching days the drivers used to refer to it as the 'white lady'.

One of the most famous of London's pubs is *Ye Olde Cheshire Cheese*, Wine Office Court, Fleet Street, which had its beginnings in the sixteenth century. Earlier, a tavern named the *Horn* stood on the site and is believed originally to have had connections with the guest house of a Carmelite monastery which disappeared at the time of the Dissolution. Certainly under the present name it has been in business through sixteen reigns and has for long been the particular haunt of literary men. Its fifteen visitors' books contain, among others, the signatures of Charles Dickens, Thackeray and, of course, Doctor Johnson.

One of the cellars of this old building extends beneath the offices of the 'Daily Telegraph', and the arches of the vaults confirm the belief that this part of the cellars was once the chapel of the guest house.

Among the inn's famous relics is the stuffed parrot, Polly which, in the forty years it lived at *Ye Olde Cheshire Cheese*, entertained visitors with its clever talk and mimicry. Its achievements included kissing Princess Mary and ordering whisky for Stanley Baldwin. So famous was the bird that when it died in 1926, the news was broadcast by the BBC and obituary notices appeared in some 200 newspapers all over the world. Nearly fifty years were to pass before a successor was presented to the tavern to take its place. The new 'Polly' was presented by the Urban District Council of Rhyl (North Wales). An African grey parrot, it is said to speak Welsh.

Unusually named is the *Woodin's Shades* at 212 Bishopsgate, London. Originally it was numbered 53 Bishopsgate Without and was the property of a wholesale tea dealer but when, in 1863, William Woodin, a beer retailer, took it over, he gave it his name. Four years later a firm of wine merchants acquired the premises, but by 1877 the name had reverted to *Woodin's Shades* and, despite many subsequent changes of ownership, so it has remained.

Luton's main industries are concerned with wheels of every description, so that the naming of a new inn on a housing estate there was almost automatic—it became the *Man on Wheels*.

The housing estate, at Hockwell Ring, Luton (Beds), was started some twenty-five years ago, but the inn was not opened until 1970. Hockwell Ring is reputed to be derived from Hocktide, a day of revels to which our forefathers were particularly addicted. Sporting activities were the main entertainment, when the Lutonians made a ring round those taking part. Needless to say, hock ales were freely imbibed.

On the main road between Settle (Yorks) and Kendal (Cumb) is the hamlet of Nether Burrow which boasts an inn with the name of *Whoop Hall*. In the thirteenth century the manor was owned by the De Burgh or Burrow family, whose home was on the site of the present inn, parts of which may date from the fifteenth and sixteenth centuries. Later the place was known as Upp Hall, a shortening of Upper Hall. The nearby house, Burrow Hall, was in 1650 known as the Low Hall.

Upp Hall was at that time owned by Christopher Pickard, who lived at a house a mile down the road at Cowan's Bridge and was a keen huntsman, with his own pack of hounds. Pickard's tenant at Upp Hall felt that to give his inn a name associated with hunting would bring him more custom, and so it became *Whoop Hall*, and remains so to this day. For over a century the property was owned by the trustees of Long Preston hospital. Turnstall church register only once refers to *Whoop Hall* and that in 1794.

Pickard's house, now known as Brontë Cottages, bears a plaque recording that it was once the residence of the Brontë sisters, and in 1824 Maria, Elizabeth, Charlotte and Emily are known to have attended a school run by a clergyman at Cowan's Bridge.

The *Lord Bexley*, Bexleyheath (Kent), has a

sign which bears the coat of arms of Nicholas Vansittart (1756–1851), who became first Baron Bexley in 1823. Although he possessed no special qualifications, he held the office of Chancellor of the Exchequer for twelve of the most difficult years in England's history during the Pitt administration. He was the first man in government to summon Nathan Meyer Rothschild to the assistance of the Treasury. Perhaps it is also to his credit that, in his last budget, he reduced the tax on salt from fifteen pence to two pence per cwt.

The *Crown & Treaty*, Uxbridge (Middx), derives its name from the fact that, in 1645, during the Civil War, Charles I and the Parliamentarians met there to negotiate a treaty, but without result. At that time the mansion was the seat of the Bennet family and was quite a large building. In 1816, much reduced in size, it became the *Crown* inn.

In the thirties the Jacobean panelling in the 'treaty' room was purchased by an American and put on exhibition in a New York art gallery. It later adorned the office of a Dr Hammer in the Empire State Building. In 1953, he wrote to HM the Queen offering to return it to England, and in due course it was exhibited at the Victoria & Albert Museum. In 1959, when the Treaty House was being repaired, the Queen's permission was obtained for the return of the panelling and now, after many travels, it is again restored to its original position.

In the village of Mereclough, nr Burnley (Lancs), the *Fighting Cocks* inn commemorates a famous cockfight. The story goes that in the days when it was customary for the local gentry to take part in the favourite sport of cockfighting, an exciting match had been arranged between the Towneleys and the Ormerods, each of whom possessed a bird famous throughout the countryside. Large sums of money were staked on these birds, so much so that tradition has it that the fate of the Ormerod estates depended upon the issue.

In the presence of a great crowd of farmers and gentry, the cocks were unbagged and round after round was fought, until at at length Butterfly, the champion of the Ormerods, lay on the ground, seemingly dying, whilst Caesar, the Towneley favourite, in little better condition, was declared the victor. Ormerod, thinking himself ruined, mounted his horse and rode towards home, but had not gone far, when he was recalled by one of his retainers shouting: 'Come back, Butterfly's

won.' With a final spasmodic effort, the bird had driven its spur into its opponent's head and so gained the victory. The name of the inn was changed that night to the *Fighting Cocks,* and for years after the sign bore on one side a picture of two cocks preparing to fly at each other with the couplet:

For heaps of gold and silver we do fight
Death comes at every blow when it hits right.

On the other side was a cock crowing over the dead body of its rival, with the words:

Brave Townley's Caesar here doth bleeding lye,
Kill'd by Ormerod's gallant Butterfly.

The boundary line between Hampshire and Wiltshire runs right through the *Red Lion,* West Dean, Salisbury (Wilts), and the licensee pays rates to both county authorities. Whilst this may be something of a nuisance, it has at least two advantages for there are two dustbin collections each week and the licensee has the choice of voting in either county during elections. At one time it was possible to drink half-an-hour longer in one side than the other. The line dividing the whole village of West Dean has long been an anomaly and it is expected that the Boundary Commission proposals will rectify it in due course.

The *Admiral Benbow*, Shrewsbury (Salop), commemorates one of the town's heroes, Admiral of the Blue John Benbow (1635–1702), the son of a local tanner. His distinguished career culminated in a mutiny which was without equal in the annals of the navy. As commander-in-chief in the West Indies in 1701, Benbow with seven ships came up with a French squadron of about equal strength. When, however, he went in to attack only two of his ships followed to support him. Heavily outnumbered in the fierce action which followed, Admiral Benbow was wounded in the face and the arm, but continued to fight on even when his leg had been shattered by grapeshot and he had to direct the battle from a hammock.

When, eventually, he reached Jamaica with his badly-mauled ship, a court martial was immediately held and two captains were sentenced to death. They were later shot on a ship in Plymouth Sound. A third captain, found to have been drunk and incapable during the action, was dismissed the Service and for good measure, also sent to prison.

In Jamaica, Admiral Benbow's shattered leg was

amputated but he died of a fever a few days afterwards, and was buried on the island. Although few could have been more deserving of the honour than the gallant admiral, it was not until 150 years after his death that the name of the *Talbot* inn, Shrewsbury, was changed to that of the *Admiral Benbow*. He also attained that pinnacle of fame reserved for heroes in the eighteenth century, a ballad to recount his deeds. It still survives:

Brave Benbow lost his legs by chain shot;
Brave Benbow lost his legs.
And all on his stumps he begs:
Fight on, my English lads, 'tis our lot.

The surgeon dressed his wounds; cries Benbow:
Let a cradle now in haste
On the quarter-deck be placed,
That the enemy I may face till I die.

At one period of his life, the admiral lived at Milton (Berks), where his daughter married a local man. There is also an *Admiral Benbow* in this village.

The *Bombay Grab*, Bow Road, London, E3, takes its name from a three-masted ship which sailed to India in 1734, with the first cargo of beer ever exported to India. The beer was brewed at the Bow brewery.

A good instance of a sign commemorating a local event is that of the *Furnham* inn, just outside Chard (Som). A canal horse used for towing barges is pictured, with a barge passing down the canal in the background. It recalls that the village of Furnham was the centre of a busy area in the mid-nineteenth century when the Chard canal was opened. It was built for small tub boats which were raised and towed on wheels up inclines, to reach different levels in sections of the canal. Thirteen-and-a-half miles long, the canal was commenced in 1834 and completed eight years later. The cost, estimated to be £57,000, actually ran up to £140,000. As the works neared Chard in 1840, a number of Chard inhabitants applied for spirit licences for inns near the terminus in anticipation of a thriving trade. They were all refused until, in 1841, a licence was granted to the *Furnham*, near to the basin and wharves.

The canal never paid its way and the advent of the railways settled its fate. It was purchased by the Bristol & Exeter Railway for £5,945 and closed in 1867. There are few visible remains of the operation except, perhaps, the rings in the wall to which the canal horses were tethered, and now the sign of the *Furnham*.

The name of the *Nobody* inn, Doddiscombsleigh (Devon), is usually reckoned to have been thought up by a wit, but there is a legend which centres round a former owner who, because of the inn's then isolated position, was careful to lock all doors and windows when the day was done. On one occasion some weary travellers hammered on the door late at night and, hearing no sound within, reluctantly moved on in the belief that nobody was in. They told their story when they did eventually find hospitality and the name *Nobody* inn stuck.

Present-day telephone callers are often somewhat disconcerted when they ring the inn and the voice at the other end asserts—'*Nobody* inn'.

The village of Lytchett Matravers, Poole (Dorset), derives its name from the English word 'letoceto'—grey wood—and a Norman family, the Matravers, who were given the estate by a grateful 'Conqueror'. The ruling squire in the fourteenth century was Sir John Matravers, one of the knights responsible for the murder of Edward II in Berkeley Castle. After the deed he fled to Germany, but was later pardoned and returned to his estate in 1365. After his death, the estate passed by marriage to the Duke of Arundel (fourth Duke of Norfolk) and he eventually sold it to the Trenchard family.

In the village is the *Chequers* inn and its name and sign come from the chequered battle flag of the Arundels, believed to be at least 400 years old. The old inn has suffered many vicissitudes, including a fire which destroyed the thatched roof, but perhaps the greatest indignity was when the historic meaning of the chequers was ignored and a new sign was hung showing two medieval gentlemen playing checkers. However, the infamy was corrected and the sign now conforms with tradition. Alas, the lounge and tiny wine bar are now all that remain of the original medieval walls and smoke-grimed oak beams, but another old tradition is still very much alive. For centuries back, country wines like parsnip, cowslip and sloe, were fermented and sold locally, and although under present licensing laws such wines have to be commercially produced and approved products, the *Chequers* still keeps a large cellar of old English country wines.

Quite a number of inns portrayed by Charles Dickens in his novels have been identified, and the *Kings Head*, Chigwell (Essex), is the 'Maypole' of

'Barnaby Rudge'. The inn, however, has another claim for fame, as in the nineteenth century the Forest Courts were held there. In one room was housed the great chest which contained the documents connected with the Verderers' Court. In 1845 it was described as the White House, Great House, or Kings Head, with the licensed premises confined to some adjoining cottages. After a few years, the *Kings Head* again became an inn of some importance, patronised by city merchants and bankers who had country houses in Essex.

The *Bun Shop*, Cambridge, was opened in 1902 by a wine and spirit merchant for the benefit of the workmen engaged in building the university museum opposite. Possibly buns and other snacks were supplied in addition to drinks at that period. Certainly for many years now hot-cross buns have been given away on Good Friday, a custom started as an advertising gimmick soon after it was opened. A bun was given with each pint of beer sold.

Unfortunately, the *Bun Shop* is due for demoli-

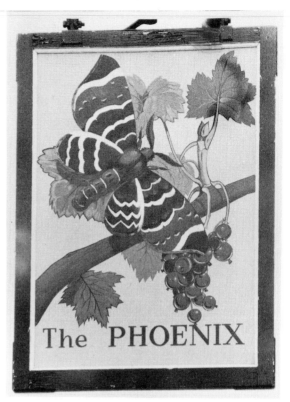

The attractive sign of another Courage house at Harlow New Town (Essex)

The sign on a Courage house at Harlow New Town (Essex) where all the inns are named after butterflies or moths. The reverse depicts a ferocious tom-cat

tion as part of a re-development scheme, but it is to be hoped that both the name and the custom will survive elsewhere.

It was a delightful departure from general practice when, on the suggestion of Dr Stephen J. L. Taylor (now Lord Taylor of Harlow), it was decided in 1951 that all new licensed premises in Harlow New Town (Essex) should be named after butterflies and moths.

Each sign bears a picture of a species of butterfly or moth on one side, and on the other a pun on the name. Typical is the *Garden Tiger*, on the reverse side of which is depicted a ferocious tom-cat. The *Small Copper* carries on the reverse a reproduction of a farthing.

Names already in use in Harlow are:

Essex Skipper	Heart & Club
White Admiral	Phoenix
Small Copper	Willow Beauty
Garden Tiger	Golden Swift
Painted Lady	Poplar Kitten
Purple Emperor	Humming Bird
Orange Footman	Drinker Moth
Shark	

The sign of the *Small Copper* at Harlow New Town (Essex) carries on the reverse a reproduction of a farthing

first British prisoner to escape from a German prison camp, and Oliver Philpot, MC, DFC, one of those who escaped through the famous 'wooden horse' in Stalag-Luft III. In the bar of the inn is a fine collection of escapers' equipment including false passports, clothes, disguises and suchlike.

A tribute to escapees from prison camps in the last war. Near Euston Station, London

Mrs Marjorie Jeffery, the licensee's wife, has most effectively given the *Victualling Office*, Stonehouse, Plymouth (Devon) a distinctive Victorian atmosphere. The inn stands close to the naval victualling yard, so that it is easy to recall the days of the Victorian navy when Britannia really ruled the waves. Items on show include a souvenir scarf, a matelot's sea chest and its contents, including two cholera belts and two pairs of flannel drawers. There are elegant chandeliers, valentine cards and a painting on glass given to Mrs Jeffery's mother by a man who was about to join the ill-fated White Star liner *Titanic*, lost with 1,500 people when she struck an iceberg in 1912.

An inn named the *Escape* might suggest a refuge from life's irritations and troubles, but the Whitbread inn of that name at Mabledon Place, near Euston Station, London, was so called for quite different reasons. This is made clear by the sign which depicts a prisoner-of-war camp with the barbed wire broken. The *Escape*, in fact, is a tribute to the hundreds of British servicemen who escaped from various camps during the 1939–45 war. The sign was unveiled by two famous escapers, Air Vice-Marshal H. Burton, CBE, DSO, the

The *Royal Oak*, Barking (Essex) is an old-established inn which has recently been completely renovated. The face-lift, however, has not caused it to lose its affectionate nickname of the 'Fly House', which it gained years ago when a large refuse dump in a field nearby was the happy hunting-ground of swarms of flies during warm weather. The new sign has a model of a fly on top of a steeple.

The *Three Kings*, Sandwich (Kent) has as its sign three portraits of Charles I. It is based upon the triple portraits by Van Dyck, now in Windsor Castle, which were sent to Bernini, the Italian sculptor, to serve as a model for a bust of the 'martyred' king.

An eighteenth-century rogue is to this day remembered by an inn named after him, the *High-wayman*, Skelmersdale New Town, near Liverpool (Lancs).

Lyon, famous for holding up the Liverpool–Wigan stage coach at Tawd Bridge, was born close to the site of the new inn. Working at first as a linen weaver, he fell among thieves and turned to crime. With his companions, Bennett and Houghton, he planned his daring robberies at the *Legs of Man* inn, which was rumoured to have been connected by a secret passage with a nearby respectable house. He was eventually caught in 1786, tried and sentenced to death, but gained a reprieve and was transported instead for seven years. His exile in the colonies failed to reform him and on his return to Skelmersdale he continued his life of crime with his two accomplices. It was 1815 before justice finally caught up with George Lyon, and April of that year saw him dangling from a rope's end at Lancaster. His tomb at Up Holland parish church can still be seen.

He was the last highwayman to be hanged in England.

The *Blind Beggar* in Whitechapel Road, London, was named after the blind beggar of Bethnal Green who, according to legend, was really the rich and battle-blinded son of Simon de Montfort (1208–65), 'father' of the English Parliament. In days gone by the 'beggar' also figured on the staff of the parish beadle. In more recent years the inn figured in the criminal proceedings against the Kray brothers.

A strange contraption is illustrated on the sign of the *Bridge*, Yatton (Som). A pair of large wheels, a chain drive and a pair of horses add up to the inscription 'Impulsoria, 1850'. The story of the vehicle is that it was one of the many inventions which followed the railway frenzy in the mid-nineteenth century. The 'Illustrated London News' of 1850 stated:

This ingenious means of applying animal power to the working of railways, so as to supersede the costly locomotive engine, has lately been invented in Italy, and exhibited experimentally on the South Western railway.

The varying proportions between the diameters of the pulleys give different degrees of speed. The horses work a moving platform that is geared to the wheels, always at their usual pace, whilst the new locomotive will be able to run at any requisite speed, even at 60 mph without ever altering the usual walking pace of the horses, which are inside the 'Impulsoria' as on the floor of a room, sheltered from the weather . . . the new machine has been brought from Italy to England and deposited at the Nine Elms terminus of the South Western railway, where it may be seen working on the

line. It has been made for two horses only and they work it very well. More than thirty wagons have been already experimentally drawn by it up the very inclined line of the station. For working it up and down the station a wagon is fastened to it and it attains a speed of 7mph. It is calculated that an engine of two horses more will run at a speed superior to that of a steam engine.

. . . by the simple manner in which the horses exercise their moving power on the new machine they can easily work the usual time (commonly about eight hours a day). During these hours the 'Impulsoria' can run at least over 30 miles eight times and as four horses do not cost more than 2s each a day, it would be an expense of 8s only, instead of £6 on account of coke only, the cost of which is 6d each mile run.

The quaint little town of Rye (Sussex) has a number of historic inns, several of them dating from the fourteenth century. The *Mermaid* was a wattle daub and plaster building *circa* AD 1300 and at that time a night's lodging could be had for a penny.

Raids by the French and a disastrous fire destroyed most of the old town and with it the *Mermaid*, leaving only the cellars unscathed. The present building was erected in 1420 and, except for a brief period when it was a club, it has been an inn practically ever since. Little has altered, including the steep cobbled street on which it stands. (Picture, p13.)

In the building today are many historic items, including two copies of love songs composed by Henry VIII, the originals of which are in the British Museum.

From the *Mermaid's* cellars a tunnel ran to another old and important inn, *Ye Olde Bell*, situated in the next street and also built in 1420. The sea at that time came right up to the lower part of the town but in the eighteenth century severe storms and continual drainage accelerated the silting up of the harbour, which has left Rye way back over the vast marshes. The area proved extremely useful to the smugglers of the eighteenth century and both inns were centres for the traffic. The infamous Hawkhurst gang used both the *Bell* and the *Mermaid* for the distribution of their contraband. At the *Bell* was a finely carved revolving cupboard, which proved invaluable for the speedy disposal of smuggled goods. It now reposes in the British Museum.

The Hawkhurst gang used the *Oak & Ivy*, Hawkhurst (Kent), a few miles inland, as their headquarters and were finally brought to justice in 1749, when the ringleaders were hanged.

The 'Dairy Maid' was the name of a pair-horse coach which ran from London to Winslow and

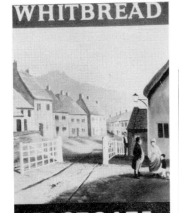

Top (*l to r*): *Ridgeway*, Newport (Mon); *Ferrie*, Symonds Yat (Herefs); *Blue Bowl*, Polsham (Som)
Centre (*l to r*): *Furnham*, Chard (Som); *Haw Bridge*, Tirley (Glos); *Wicor*, Portchester (Hants)
Bottom (*l to r*): *Eastgate*, Cowbridge (Glam); *Shutter*, Gotherington (Glos); *Avondale*, Devonport (Devon)

Buckingham, passing through Aylesbury en route. It became especially famous when it carried the news of the victory at Waterloo to Aylesbury on 20 June 1815, just two days after the battle. The news was received in London thirty hours after the victory.

An account written in 1897 reads:

There are many events worthy of remembrance in my long life which seem almost incredible. I have heard my father describe the announcement of the Battle of Waterloo with its effects on him, and the recollection of it is so vivid, I seem somehow to have been with him myself.

He said that on June 20, in that memorable year, 1815, he was haymaking on the meadow at the back of his premises about midday, when he heard his name shouted out, and leaning on his hayfork, he observed the driver of the 'Dairy Maid'. The coachman was an old friend of my family and he it was who addressed my father, who wasn't then twenty-three years of age, as 'Master John, I bring you great news, and no one in Aylesbury shall know it before you. Bonyparte and all his French army are destroyed: the Duke of Wellington, God bless him! has fought and beat him at a place called Waterloo.'

My father told me he was so overcome with joy, for he had lived all his life in war, that he involuntarily fell down on his knees in the hayfield and thanked God for what he at once saw was the blessing of peace. The coachman had hurried back, when he found the horses had been changed, and fixing blue ribbons on their heads and a big bow on his whip, drove triumphantly through the town, telling everyone the startling news.

So, in 1966, this historic occasion and famous coach were remembered when the Aylesbury Brewery opened a new inn and named it the *Dairy Maid*. Features of the decor are a large, coloured, mosaic panel illustrating the coach, and a mural showing it passing through the Chilterns at night. The exterior sign, a three-sided one, also features the 'Dairy Maid' coach.

There are six *Boot* inns in Buckinghamshire, three in Bedfordshire and one in Huntingdonshire, and all enquiries about them lead one to the legend attaching to a monk, John Schorne, who came from Monks Risborough to be vicar of North Marston, a village near Winslow (Bucks). He was a very pious man and it was said that his knees became horny from the frequency of his prayers.

Towards the end of the thirteenth century, the area is said to have suffered from a series of droughts so severe that the earth became scorched, cattle died and all the wells dried up. Additional torments the villagers were called upon to bear were plagues of fleas, flies and gnats. Taking pity on the plight of his parishioners John Schorne struck the caked earth with his staff and immediately a spring of crystal clear water welled up from the earth.

The fame of the chalybeate mineral water, not less the way it was miraculously conjured from the ground, spread far and wide and when it was found to have healing properties, especially for the ague, Schorne's spring very soon became a holy well. For the accommodation of pilgrims and sufferers houses after the style of inns were built.

No one knows the circumstances which led this pious man to conjure the devil into a boot, but this was held to have been his greatest achievement, and round the wall of the well were the words:

Sir John Schorne,
Gentleman borne,
Conjured the Devil into a boot.

The 'Sir' being a medieval courtesy for rectors. When he died in 1314, his will bequeathed:

What is God's to God, his soul;
What is earth's to earth, his body;
His goods partly to his orators and partly to the poor who were to bear the goods to heaven with their own hands where John Schorne might find them again.

A rood screen at Suffield (Norfolk) includes a figure of Sir John holding a boot (more like a stocking) with a winged devil peering from the top, and pilgrims' signs with the same motif have been found in the Thames at Queenhithe. There is still a Schorn Lane at North Marston.

As for the well, it continued to supply the village with water until recent years, but when the mains supply reached North Marston it was ignominiously covered by a concrete slab. Now efforts are being made to reinstate the well as a memorial to the saintly man who was the village rector some seven hundred years ago.

The *Boot* is by no means rare elsewhere in the British Isles, where it is usually attributed to St Crispin—patron saint of cobblers. There is a *Crispin* at Woolaston (Northants).

One of the 'Station Hotels' to lose its identity under the Beeching 'axe' was that at Isfield (Sussex). The inn dates back a hundred years and stood alongside the Lewes–Uckfield line. When the line closed the name was obviously no longer appropriate and as it then served as the headquarters of the local angling club the brewers, Beard & Co (Lewes), consulted members about an alternative name. By common consent the inn was renamed the *Laughing Fish*.

On the east coast of Fife (Scotland), there are a number of quaint little seaports which a Scottish king once referred to as the 'golden tassels to the beggar's mantle'. Anstruther, or Anster, was the 'capital' of this diminutive kingdom and here for three centuries or more has been a noted inn, the *Smugglers*. In the Jacobite rising of 1715, the Pretender was proclaimed there by the Earl of Strathmore, and each year the inn was the head-quarters for revellers at the annual games. A more sombre side to its history was its association with smugglers bringing their contraband over from France, and a passage from the inn once led to some inland hide-out.

The *Smugglers* still survives on the very edge of the small burn which flows between Wester and Easter Anstruther.

Rich indeed in history is the *Rothley Court*, near Rothley (Leics). Formerly an ancient Leicestershire mansion, it was the country seat of Lord Macaulay's brother-in-law, and here in the temple Thomas Babington Macaulay, statesman, philosopher and poet, was born in 1800. William Wilberforce stayed at the house as a guest while he drafted the Act of Parliament which abolished slavery in 1807.

But its real history dates back to the twelfth century when the chapel at Rothley Court was given to the Knights Templar, an order of knight-hood which was started in the year 1118 by nine French knights, who took an oath of poverty, chastity and obedience. They were known as the poor knights because they had no income and were dependent on charity. At one period they even had to make do with one horse between two knights. The order was founded for the protection of pil-grims on their way to the holy sepulchre at Jeru-salem but the knights also waged perpetual war against the infidels. They wore a white mantle on which was superimposed a red cross as a sign of their constant exposure to martyrdom.

The fame of their valiant deeds in the Holy Land spread all over the civilised world and soon the sons of the nobility flocked to their standard. In England they first established themselves at Hol-born, in London, in 1185. When they came into possession of the temple at Rothley, Henry III instructed that his body should be buried there but, in the event, he was buried in Westminster Abbey.

The order became wealthy, powerful and even-tually so corrupt that it was abolished in Europe

Isles of Scilly

and its members persecuted with great cruelty. In England, the order was suppressed in 1312.

Another famous visitor to Rothley was Queen Elizabeth in 1560.

During alterations at Rothley Court, several skeletons over 300 years old were found and re-buried in the grounds of the chapel.

The *Loggerheads*, Gwernymynydd (Flintshire) is sometimes referred to as the 'Three Logger-heads' because the signboard depicts two men's heads back to back and, below, the lettering 'We three loggerheads'. When the unwary visitor asked where the third was, he was told 'He's inside, having one!' There is little doubt that the original sign was painted by a founder member of the Royal Academy, Richard Wilson, who was the son of a Welsh clergyman and born nearby the inn, but when he painted it is very uncertain. He left home for London when sixteen years of age and by the 1740s was a noted portrait painter in London. Later he went to Italy, where he gained respect for his landscapes.

Wilson revisted his birthplace several times and it was possibly on one of these occasions that the innkeeper, a tenant of Wilson's cousin, bemoaned his lack of a sign, whereupon the artist good naturedly sat down and amused himself by painting this humorous sign. Some years ago, an itinerant artist offered to restore the work to its original freshness but unfortunately did it some harm. The inn is some 400 years old and was previously a coach-house.

A sign painted by another famous landscape artist, David Cox, is now preserved inside the *Royal Oak*, Bettws-y-Coed (Caerns).

At St Mary's, Isles of Scilly, is the *Bishop & Wolf*, appropriately named after the Wolf Rock and Bishops Rock lighthouses. The first of these is off the islands and was established in 1840, the present structure being completed twenty-nine years later. The tower stands 135ft high. The Bishops Rock is at the extreme south-west of the islands and occupies one of the most exposed posi-tions of any lighthouse in the world. The granite tower is 163ft high. The inn sign is two-sided and portrays on one side a mitred bishop with a model of a lighthouse in his hand and, on the reverse, a fearsome-looking wolf crouching above the light-house. (Picture, p41.)

Also at St Mary's is the *Star Castle*, named after the castle which was built in 1593 for the defence of the islands. In 1643 it sheltered the prince, after wards Charles II, from the ships of Parliament, and

later was the headquarters of Sir John Grenville, the Royalist privateer. The castle was the last stronghold of the Royalist troops.

Today, the eight-pointed building serves as a hotel, but is still surrounded by a dry moat and 18ft-broad ramparts. The great kitchen fireplace, where oxen were once roasted whole, is still to be seen.

A triple murder which took place in 1734 is recalled by the *Royal Oak*, Wivelsfield, near Hay-wards Heath (Sussex). The original inn was the setting for this macabre event when late one night Jacob Harris, a Jewish pedlar and a regular visitor to the inn, roused the landlord, Richard Miles, who got up and took the pedlar's horse to the stables. There Harris attacked Miles, cutting his throat, and when the disturbance roused the serv-ing maid, she was similarly attacked and murdered. Harris then returned to the inn, murdered Miles's wife in her bed and plundered the building. On returning to the stables, Harris found that Miles had vanished, and promptly fled in panic. Miles meanwhile had managed to reach help and give a description of his assailant but died within a few days.

Three days later, Harris was arrested, convicted at Horsham Assizes and executed in the town. His body was brought back and hung on a gibbet on Ditchling Common to serve as a deterrent, the usual practice of the time. Local people believed that wooden splinters from the gibbet were a remedy for many common ailments, particularly toothache.

The gibbet remained on Ditchling Common until, towards the end of the nineteenth century, its rotting remains were replaced by the present post, surmounted by a metal cockerel perforated with the date '1734'. The post is now protected by a triangular wooden fence.

At one time the 'port way' meant the way to the town and this is the name given to an inn at Staunton-on-Wye (Herefordshire). The sign of the *Portway* is excellent, showing a patient packhorse jogging into market with master and child seated among the eggs and vegetables. A gay note is struck by the flowers which the master grasps, obviously intended for someone special.

The unusual name of the *Duke without a Head*, Wateringbury (Kent) is said to derive from the time when the inn replaced the old *Duke's Head* nearby, which was demolished. 'Permission is given to remove the Duke's Head', the order stated, and so was added yet another oddity to the names of inns. The sign shows the bust of a coroneted peer in morning dress and wearing a flower in his buttonhole.

At the *Fox & Hounds*, Hungerford Bottom (Hants), there is a very fine collection of old agricultural implements. The proprietor of the inn purchased an old tithe barn and rebuilt it at the rear of the place, where it now serves as a most interesting museum.

A humorous sign at Banwell (Som)

The *Drunken Duck*, Hawkshead (Lancs) is well known and was recently joined by a *Whistling Duck*, whose humorous and attractive sign will no doubt become equally popular. It adorns a new house, which was opened at Banwell, near Weston-super-Mare (Som), in 1967. To find a popular name for the inn, a competition was run in the local newspaper and of the many ingenious suggestions the 'Whistling Duck', suggested by an eight-year-old girl, was chosen. The sign depicts a cheerful bird strutting along and whistling, the notes ballooning from its beak.

There are many inns bearing the name *Hop Pole* and the sign of the one at Cheltenham (Glos) reminds us of the days—not long past— when hops were trained up stout poles and not, as now, on wires. Hops were not in general use in Europe until the fourteenth century, and aromatic herbs were used instead to give flavour and longer life to beer. (Pictures, p75.)

At Midsummer Common, Cambridge (Cambs), *The Fort St George in England* bears a name which has been held by an inn on an island site in the river Cam since 1520. The lock gates nearby were operated by earlier tenants until the late 1800s. Due to its island situation, it is believed that the inn was likened to Fort St George in Madras, but to avoid any misunderstanding, 'in England' was added. A sketch of the inn dated 1812 carries the full name but it is only recently that its use has been resumed. The sign, which is of recent design, depicts an old fort with ships approaching.

There is only one inn named the *Dog Tray* and this is at Brighton (Sussex). The name was inspired by a German poem about a dog named Tray. The verses carved on a plaque above the bar of the inn speak for themselves:

The Trough was full and faithful Tray
Came out to drink one sultry day.
He wagged his tail and wet his lip
When cruel Fred snatched up a whip.
And whipped poor Tray till he was sore
And kicked and whipped him more and more.

At this good Tray grew very red
And growled and bit him till he bled
Then you should only have been by
To see how Fred did scream and cry.

So Frederick had to go to bed his leg was very
    sore and red.
The doctor came and shook his head
And made a very great todo
And gave him nasty physic too.

But good 'Dog Tray' is happy now
He has no time to say bow wow.
He seats himself in Frederick's chair
And laughs to see the nice things there
And soup he swallows sup by sup
And eats the pies and puddings up.

The 'Dog Tray' must once have been famous for in an old music hall bill of 100 years ago it was billed as a popular sketch.

Adjacent to the post office in the Cotswold town of Stroud (Glos) is the *Post Office*. The Concorde

43

frequently flies over the town as it takes-off from nearby Fairford aerodrome, and the inn's highly topical sign shows the Concorde stamp and post-mark on an envelope. (Picture, p31.)

The *Snowcat*, Cambridge (Cambs), is named after the vehicle used with such great success on the Trans-Antarctic expedition of 1957–58, as a result of which Sir Vivian Fuchs, the leader, became the first man to traverse the Antarctic, covering 2,200 miles in ninety-nine days. It was he who officially opened the *Snowcat*. Cleverly defined in the pro-file of the inn is the shape of the vehicle, informa-tion about it is on display in the bars, and the sign shows a 'snowcat' ploughing through the Arctic wastes.

In Porchester (Hants) is the *Cormorant*, an inn which was rebuilt on the site of the old *Swan*. The story goes that a cormorant flying over was shot down and plummetted to earth right outside the inn, whereupon the name was changed.

The *Dimsdale Arms*, Hertford (Herts), is associ-ated with a local family who originally came from Essex, but by the eighteenth century had put down their roots in Hertford. Thomas Dimsdale (1720–1800) trained as a doctor at St Thomas's hospital, London, and then quickly established himself in private practice. During the rebellion of 1745, he offered his services to the Duke of Cumberland and travelled to Carlisle. Later he was a pioneer of vaccination against smallpox and his fame spread.

He accepted an invitation to St Petersburg from Catherine the Great to vaccinate both herself and her son. The Empress had great faith in him, but she was not so sure how her subjects might react should anything go wrong. She therefore arranged for post horses to be stationed right across her dominions so that the doctor's flight could be instant and rapid. In the event all went well, especially for Dimsdale who was paid a fee of £10,000, and given a £500 annuity and £2,000 in expenses. In addition, he was created a Baron of the Empire of all the Russias with the right to add a wing of the black Russian eagle to his fam-ily coat of arms. Both Thomas and his son, Nathan-iel, represented Hertford in Parliament. Thomas was married three times and was eventually buried in the Quakers' cemetery at Bishop's Stortford. The local church of St Andrew contains a memorial tablet eulogising the family's accomplishments in forty-two lines of praise.

The inn, however, was not always the *Dimsdale Arms*. Originally the *Red Lion*, it became the *Half Moon* and then the *Duncombe Arms*. It acquired its present name in 1833 and the sign is emblazoned with the Dimsdale arms, including, of course, the wing of the Russian eagle.

As far back as 1780 there was an alehouse attached to the bakehouse at North End, Little Yeldham (Essex). A fire of faggots heated the stones on which the bread was baked, and when the ale-house was promoted to an inn, it became the *Stone & Faggot*. The place was burnt down in 1914, but rebuilt a year later. The name would appear to be unique as that of an inn.

The Barber-Surgeons Company of London pos-sess a remarkable loving cup that was presented to them by Charles II. At the Restoration, the king intended to form a new order of chivalry, equivalent to the Order of the Bath, and for this purpose caused several Oak Tree cups to be pre-pared. The Order, however, never materialised and instead the cups were presented.

The cup of silver and silver-gilt, known as the Oak Tree cup, has a stem and body resembling an oak tree and from it hang acorns fashioned as bells, which ring as it is passed from hand to hand round the festive board on special occasions. The cover represents the royal crown of England and engraved around it on four plaques are the Barber-Surgeon's shield and crest with three Latin inscriptions. It is hallmarked 'London 1676' and, altogether, it is a very handsome piece of work. The Latin engrav-ing reads:

Presented to John Knight, Principal Surgeon to the King, and James Pearce in the Year when Scarburgh was the Master. The gift of the most munificent King Charles II in the year 1676.

Sir Charles Scarburgh was chief physician to his Majesty, as well as master of the company.

It was a happy thought of the signboard artist, Stanley Chew, to use this as a variation of the Royal Oak theme of which there are hundreds up and down the country. This interesting sign now swings at the *Royal Oak*, Clevedon (Som).

Few inns situated in such a relatively quiet back-water have seen industrial history made on the scale witnessed by the riverside *Ship* inn, Mor-wellham, on the Tamar just nineteen miles north of Plymouth (Devon).

Its story dates back to the fourteenth century and from the sixteenth to the eighteenth century the port thrived on shipment of the tin and other ores in which the country around Tavistock was

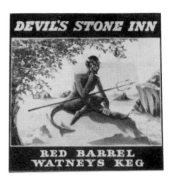

Left: *The Park,*
Exmouth (Devon)

Right: The
Devil's Stone,
Shebbear (Devon)

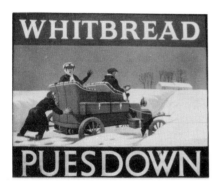

The two sides of the sign of the *Puesdown* (Glos)

Left: *The Gaydons,*
Barnstaple (Devon)

Right: *Cheese Rollers,*
Shurdington (Glos)

remarkably rich. It was however, in the mid-nineteenth century that the traffic reached its peak, following a number of fabulously rich strikes of copper in the area. The Wheal Maria, Wheal Fanny and a number of other mines sprang up in rapid succession, and eventually were all melded to become the Devonshire Great Consolidated Mining Company. There seemed no limit to their output or to the company's prosperity. A £1 share often brought enough dividend for a man to buy a house. The record bonus was in 1846, when £71 per £1 share was paid.

Earlier, the Tavistock canal had been built to ease the problems of transport from the mines to the port. So great were the difficulties and so unyielding the granite through which the miners had to tunnel, that the canal took seventeen years to build. Then, as Morwellham became overwhelmed with the ever-increasing traffic, new quays and a railway were built to speed the flow of ore down to the 300-ton schooners which carried it over to South Wales for smelting.

The copper boom lasted well into the 1860s and then, as so often has been the case in Britain, the bottom suddenly fell out of the whole business. To some extent arsenic took the place of the copper and prolonged activity in the area for about twenty years, after which that trade also ceased.

Morwellham then went to sleep and gradually the port and its installations fell into disuse and decay. It was a slumber undisturbed for nearly 100 years and then, largely through a fascinating book dealing with the archaeology of Cornwall by a Plymouth man, Frank Booker, the Dartington Hall Amenity Research Trust began to clean up the site and by conservation, and the provision of facilities for recreation and study, aroused interest in the remarkable history of this almost forgotten little port.

Today it is again thriving, and a centre of interest to visitors who come from far and near. The old inn still stands, now far more respectable than it could ever have been in its rough mining days when the tea room, which now caters for present-day visitors, was no doubt put to the service of stronger brews.

When, in 1970, the *Marquis of Cornwallis* in Collier Street, Finsbury, London, was demolished, one of the remaining links with the famous clown, Joseph Grimaldi, disappeared.

Coming from a family of clowns and dancers, he made his mark at the age of three and later starred at both Sadlers Wells and Drury Lane theatres. At one period he appeared at both places each night,

running from one to the other between performances. It was a mode of life that exacted its toll on his health and in 1837, when he was forty, he was taken ill, his condition gradually deteriorated and be became paralysed from the waist down. In his retirement, he met his friends regularly at the *Marquis of Cornwallis*, and was drinking there one night when he became unwell. The landlord carried him back to his home close by but next morning he died at the age of fifty-eight. History records that he had no equal in his profession, his grimaces alone often stopping the show.

Another famous clown of our own day has recently had the lounge of a public house named after him. The inn is the *White Swan* at Woodnewton (Northants) where Coco's Lounge honours Coco the Clown, otherwise Nicolai Polokovs, who lives in the village and is a regular at the pub.

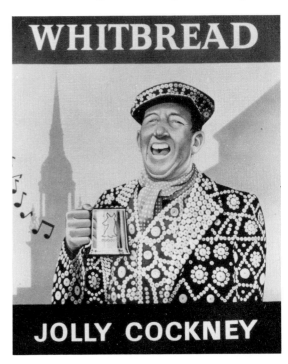

Another lively and appropriate sign at Lambeth, London

For centuries, the *Three Tuns*, just by the famous Banbury Cross in the Oxfordshire town of Banbury, was an important inn. The Banbury Cross is traditionally associated with the nursery rhyme 'Ride a Cock Horse', which refers to the ancient May Day festival, a relic of primitive fertility rites. The 'fine lady' with rings on her fingers and bells on her toes was the earth goddess, personified by a nude girl riding upon a white horse.

She was accompanied by youths and maidens singing and dancing and strewing flowers as they made their way in slow procession to the cross where a maypole was set up, representing the sacred tree. The rest of the day was spent in dancing round it, in sports and feasting, and eating the mystical Beltane cakes.

The famous Puritan divine, William Whately, was born at the parsonage opposite the inn in 1583. At the age of fourteen, he went to Cambridge where he quickly won a reputation as an orator before studying for the ministry and later, in 1610, being appointed to the living at Banbury. None too popular at first because of his puritan outlook, his fame soon spread and he was much sought after as a preacher all over the Midlands. His style of preaching was typically puritan, being theatrical and rhetorical, and with his able body and sound lungs he earned for himself the sobriquet of 'the roaring boy of Banbury'.

In 1619, he published 'A Bride Bush', or a direction for married persons, plainly describing the duties common to both and peculiar to each of them. It raised such a storm of opposition in the Church that he was convened before the high commission but, on his retracting his propositions, the charge was dismissed.

Whately died in 1639 and, presumably, it was shortly afterwards that the *Three Tuns* was renamed *Whately Hall* in acknowledgement of his popularity.

The area outside the inn was for some five centuries the scene of the renowned Banbury horse fairs, which drew keen-eyed dealers from all over the country. It was during the horse fair of 1742 that one of the last public hangings took place in the town. A widow, Lydia Wile, had been brutally murdered in the cellar of her house a few yards away from the inn by a man named Parr. He was executed opposite the scene of his crime, and his body carried through the town by four chimney sweeps to the gibbet on the Oxford road.

The ancient inn forms the core of the present hotel, and a well-made stone-built underground passage leads from the cellar and across the road to Banbury Cross. It could well have once been an escape route for priests in the times of religious strife, and may later have been enlarged to serve as a culvert. One bedroom of *Whately's* today still has a priests' hidey-hole by the stone fireplace which leads to a nearby room. The vaulted cellars also remain and part of them has been converted into an excellent cocktail bar.

The *Ebrington Arms* stands in the picturesque village of that name, near Chipping Campden (Glos) and, close by the church, is Ebrington manor, where lived Sir John Fortescue, a fifteenth-century Lord Chief Justice of England. A remarkable man with an apparently iron constitution, he laid aside his gown when he was seventy years of age to fight in the battle of Towton and moreover went on fighting through the long and bitter Wars of the Roses. He eventually retired to his manor house, which still stands, where he died at the age of ninety. His tomb, surmounted by an effigy dressed in his chancellor's robes, is in the church.

The first Fortescue came to England with the Conqueror and with his shield prevented an arrow striking William during the battle of Hastings. The Conqueror's comment 'Forte écu' (strong shield), is now part of the Fortescue family motto. (Picture, p53.)

Nearly 125 years after the dismal failure of an unusual railway system, an inn at Starcross (Devon) has been named after it. Brunel's atmospheric railway was built on the western side of the river Exe in 1847 and ran for only twelve months. The story dates back to 1836 when the great engineer was carrying out a survey for a railway line from Exeter to Plymouth and it was decided to operate it by means of an atmospheric system—in short, to harness the pressure of the atmosphere as a propelling force.

The system was the invention of two brothers named Samuda, and consisted of cast-iron pipes 15in in diameter laid between the rails and in which a close-fitting piston travelled. At intervals along the route, stationary steam engines were erected to work large air-pumps so that the air could be exhausted from the pipe, thus creating a partial vacuum within. To enable the piston to be connected with the carriage to which the train was attached, a continuous slit, $2\frac{1}{2}$in wide, ran along the top of the pipe which was closed by a flap of leather. The air in the pipe in front of the piston was driven out by the stationary engines, the piston was driven forward by the atmospheric pressure behind and carried the train with it, leaving the pipe ready to be again exhausted for the next train. The method of traction was not exactly new, for it had been tried on the West London Railway between Wormwood Scrubs and Croydon and its possibilities became the subject of acute controversy among engineers of the day. George Stephenson called it 'a great humbug', whereas Brunel championed it as a scheme with immense possibilities. From an estimated £330,000, the cost soared to £426,000, and though the trains proved capable of a speed of

68mph the scheme was a failure, largely because rats persisted in eating the greased leather flaps which covered the slits in the pipes.

The pumping station at Starcross is almost the last visible evidence of the 'dream', and now, close to the line it commemorates, is the new inn sign of the *Atmospheric Railway,* a reminder of what over 100 years ago Devonshire people referred to as the 'atmospheric caper'.

In the bar of the *Atmospheric Railway* are a number of interesting photographs and reproductions concerning the great experiment.

Stepney Green, East London, home of the traditional cockney, is the obvious site for the *Pearly Queen.* In the Lambeth Road (SE1), equally appropriately, is the *Lambeth Walk,* taking its name from the nearby thoroughfare which leads from Broad Street to Lambeth Road. The name could also be in commemoration of the cockney dance which, introduced by Lupino Lane in the musical show 'Me and my Gal' in the 1940s, became popular throughout the country. Also to to be found in Lambeth is the Whitbread house, *Jolly Cockney,* whose sign depicts a 'pearly king' downing a pint within the sound of Bow Bells.

Near Reading (Berks), an inn was re-named the *Nine Saxons* after the discovery in the vicinity of a Saxon burial ground containing nine skeletons. The sign shows a Saxon warrior with the skulls at his feet.

The several *Portsmouth Arms* in North Devon take their name from the Portsmouth family, who at one time owned the land over a wide area. Their country seat was Eggesford House and in the nineteenth century Lord Portsmouth, who was a great hunting man, filled the spacious mansion with guests who hunted six days a week. He was master of hounds for thirty years and bred the hounds which provided the foundation blood for most of the great packs of today.

A great character epitomising John Bull, Lord Portsmouth was a coachman of no mean ability, and a story is told of when the family were in Paris while travelling abroad in their own four-horse coach. When they were about to leave the city the elder son, later the fifth Earl, was missing. 'Never mind,' exclaimed his Lordship, 'I'll soon get him.' Suiting the action to the word, he seized the coach horn and startled everyone in the Place Vendôme by blowing long blasts, until sure enough the missing member rejoined the party.

When the Exeter–Barnstaple railway was built

in 1854, the line was only allowed to pass through his Lordship's estate on condition that he had the right to stop trains for the convenience of himself or his guests. And when a station was built at Eggesford, all passenger trains were to stop on a signal which might be requested by *any* person desiring to travel. Close by the station still is the *Fox & Hounds,* with a very large sign showing the hunt in full cry.

At the *Portsmouth Arms,* Umberleigh (N Devon), some interesting records concerning Eggesford House and the Portsmouth family are on show, and a frequent visitor to Eggesford, the famous hunting parson, Jack Russell, is remembered by the *Jack Russell,* Swimbridge (N Devon). The sign carries a portrait of the parson, who founded the famous and popular breed of Jack Russell terriers.

The popular sign of the *Magpie & Stump* in Old Bailey, London, shows a magpie perched on a stump and the name is believed to have come from London slang. A 'magpie' was a halfpenny, and to 'stump up' still means to pay up. Possibly, however, it may be of even older origin and date back to the days when half-a-pint was known as a 'magpie'. This Old Bailey inn was a famous Whig pothouse at the time of the Gordon riots in 1715.

History was being made by customers of the *White Hart,* Biggin Hill (Kent) in the desperate early years of World War II, for it was here that many hundreds of pilots from the nearby RAF fighter station of No 11 Group, Fighter Command, used to call for a drink. When, in September 1971, the hosts of the *White Hart,* Mr and Mrs Ted Preston who had been landlords since 1932, retired, more than a hundred Battle of Britain pilots met once again to bid them farewell. Many had received much kindness and help from them in those dark days of 1940, when the fate of Britain was in the hands of 'the few'.

The *Centurion,* a new Courage inn, Bicester (Oxon), owes its name to its situation close to the old Roman walled town of Alchester, which stood at the junction of the roads leading to Lactodorum (Towcester), Verulamium (St Albans), Corinium (Cirencester) and Venta (Winchester). A fine pictorial sign shows Mars, god of war, watching from the clouds as a Roman centurion flees in terror at the approach of a twentieth-century tank.

At Bray, the east Berkshire village on the river Thames, is the *Monkey Island* hotel. The name comes from the famous monkey pictures which have

Golden Hind

SHIPS
ON
INN SIGNS

The *Ship's Tavern & King's Head*,
Plymouth (Devon)

Above: *The Golden Hind*,
Musbury (Devon)

Below: The *Royal George*,
Worcester (Worcs)

Above: The *Ship*,
Caerleon (Mon)

Below: The *Old Ship*,
Lee-on-Solent (Hants)

The *Captain Cook Inn*,
Staithes (Yorks)

adorned the domed ceiling of the monkey room since 1730. They were painted by a French artist, Andien de Clermont, when it was the fishing-lodge of the third Duke of Marlborough.

In 1971, with the aid of an £850 grant from the Department of Environment, the pictures, which had become so dark as to be hardly distinguishable, were beautifully restored, and one shows monkeys following the ever popular pastime of 'messing about in boats'.

One of the great hoaxes of this age was perpetrated by an amateur antiquarian, Charles Dawson, a Sussex lawyer. Cranial fragments which he claimed to have found at Piltdown in 1912 were at first accepted by anthropologists as a discovery of immense importance and though later on doubts arose, it was not until forty years had passed that scientific tests proved them to be a fake. The *Piltdown Man*, near Maresfield, (Sussex), is a reminder of the deception and has a sign typifying the popular conception of the 'caveman' with straight overhanging brow, extended jowl and the inevitable club.

An intriguing story is associated with the *Widow's Son*, a pub in Devons Road, Bow, in London's East End. It tells of a young fellow who, going to sea in 1824, asked his mother to save him a hot cross bun. The boy never returned but a bun was faithfully kept each year. The tradition held and in later years, when a hot cross bun was added to the collection every Good Friday, the area was searched for a sailor to partake of the inn's hospitality. That is why, still hanging from the ceiling, there is a large net bag containing buns—once hot but now exceedingly stale.

The small village of Middleton, near Heysham (Lancs), is served by the *Old Roof Tree* inn. Originally, the building was a farmhouse but in 1956 it was converted by Thwaites & Co, the Blackburn brewers, to a fine 'old-world' inn with oak-studded doorways and mullioned windows. The east part of the building was called Roof Tree Cottage, because many years ago a tree grew up through the roof. Indeed, part of the trunk may still be seen embedded in the wall.

In the seventeenth century Middleton was the local headquarters of George Fox, who founded the Society of Friends. Members of the society were severely persecuted all over the country, particularly in Lancashire, and the longest of Fox's many terms of imprisonment was spent in Lancaster jail, 1663–66. The Friends later became known as

'Quakers' and were referred to as such in the House of Commons journals of 1654. The nickname is said to have come when Fox, on trial before a bench of magistrates, bade them tremble at the word of the Lord.

Lancaster was the first British seaport to import cotton and when Glasson dock was being built, liquor was sold to the labourers engaged in the construction work from a hulk lying there known as Salisbury's Hook. Later the place became known as the *Pier Hall*, then the *Grapes* and, finally, the *Caribou* due to the owners' association with the Canadian trade. Thwaites & Co of the Star Brewery, Blackburn, have rebuilt the inn and today it is centred on a thriving scene.

In Combe Martin (N Devon), which has surely the longest street of any village in the land, is the *Royal Marine*, with a sign showing a sergeant of the corps in full-dress uniform. The Royal Marines' depot at Lympstone, near Exmouth (Devon), adopted the inn and presented the landlord with a miniature marine drum, a plaque and several old recruiting posters.

There is another *Royal Marine* at Plymouth (Devon).

Episodes in history have inspired the naming of many inns and in the North Country there are at least two which commemorate an encounter between the United States frigate 'Chesapeake' and the British frigate 'Leopard'. In 1807 the British boarded the American ship and carried off some of their seamen who had deserted from the British Navy. The episode led to a proclamation ordering British men-of-war from American waters, and also to the names of at least two North Country inns —the *Two Ships*, Todmorden (Yorks) and again at Rochdale (Lancs).

The origin of many inn names has long been the cause of heated controversy and two classic examples, each with many theories attached to it, are the *Elephant & Castle*, and the *Case is Altered*.

Another is the *Blackboys* inn, near Uckfield (E. Sussex). The building is believed to date back to the fourteenth century, and many years ago it was adjacent to an important iron foundry whose products included the cast iron railings which surround St Paul's Cathedral. The inn had many thirsty regulars from the foundry and some of the men were so begrimed with charcoal after a long stint at the furnaces that the inn is thought to have taken its name from them.

When the industry died out, the inn fell on difficult times until it gained new patronage from the farmers who brought their cattle, a Sussex breed nicknamed 'wildishers', to graze on the land round about.

On the wall of the bar is a stag's head and the ancient game of ringing the stag, is still played. The play consists of attempting to lob a bull ring over the nose of the stag, the ring being attached to a piece of fishing line suspended from one of the oak beams and just long enough to reach the stag's nose.

Several intriguing tales have been woven around this ancient inn. One is that there is a secret room in the chimney high up in the roof, though it has never yet been discovered. Another tells of a secret alcove in the side of the deep well which plunges down to a frightening blackness from the kitchen floor. It is said that innkeepers found the alcove a useful hiding-place for the kegs of brandy which smugglers brought over the downs in the midnight hours. It is not difficult to imagine in this or a hundred other ancient inns, the story behind the lines of Rudyard Kipling's 'Smuggler's Song':

> Five and twenty ponies
>   trotting through the dark—
> Brandy for the Parson
> Baccy for the Clerk
> Laces for a lady, letters for a spy
> And watch the wall my darling, while the
>   Gentlemen go by.

Another, and perhaps more valid claim, is that the name of the inn came, not from the foundry boys but from the then Lord of the Manor, Sir Philip Blakeboy.

In 1971 the *Pilot* inn, Exmouth (Devon), had for the first time a pictorial sign and what more fitting than it should carry on one side a portrait of a well-known local pilot, and on the reverse the Trinity House coat of arms? The pilot, Mr H. J. Bradford, known to his innumerable friends and acquaintances as Dido, retired after thirty-six years' solid service behind him. Crew member of the lifeboat for twenty-six years and a further six years as coxswain, he holds the bronze medal of the Royal National Lifeboat Institution for his courage, skill and determination in rescuing three people from a wrecked cabin-cruiser. Mr John Cook, responsible for so many Whitbread signs, painted the portrait from a photograph and one sitting, and it is declared an excellent likeness. The *Pilot* inn now stands some half-a-mile from the sea but there is still a highwater mark on its step to show that many years ago the sea came up to the very door of the inn. (Picture, p63.)

Richard Cobden (1804–65) is one of the many politicians, past and present, celebrated enough to have an inn named after him. He was born in a farmhouse at Heyshott, near Midhurst (Sussex) and when, in 1814, his father had to sell the farm, Richard, the fourth of eleven children, was sent to a 'Dotheboys Hall' type of school in Yorkshire. He later became a dedicated politician and in his heyday was known as the 'apostle of Free Trade' because of his strong advocacy for repeal of the Corn Laws. At the village of Cocking, at the foot of the South Downs and a mile from his birthplace, now stands the *Richard Cobden* inn, its sign carrying a portrait of the great man.

Prior to the coaching era the *Crown*, Arnside (Westmorland), was known as the *Fighting Cocks* and gained a widespread reputation as a cockfighting centre. After the so-called sport had been made illegal in 1849, surreptitious matches no doubt still took place there. Eventually the *Crown* became a coaching inn and from it, in the early nineteenth century, a stage plied between Morecambe and Heysham, and Arnside and Grange-over-Sands.

At Shurdington, near Cheltenham (Glos), is the *Cheese Rollers* with a picturesque sign depicting an annual ceremony which has been carried on at nearby Cooper's Hill for over 400 years. Tradition has it that it commemorates the inalienable rights of the local farmers and shepherds to graze their sheep on the commonland in the vicinity. In earlier days the starting point of the race was marked by a maypole at the top of the hill but now competitors assemble at a flagpole every Whit Monday to await the starter's orders. Wearing the traditional 'uniform' of a Cotswold shepherd's smock and a white beaver hat, he fires a pistol and a host of youths set off down the hill, with its gradient of 1 in 3, in pursuit of the 'Double Gloucester' cheese which has previously been released. The object of the exercise is to overtake the cheese, nowadays an imitation protected by a stout casing, before it reaches the bottom of the hill. The victor —the first to reach the bottom, for the cheese is rarely caught—receives a cheese and a small money prize. (Picture, p45.)

William Hunter of Brentwood was a Protestant victim of religious intolerance in the sixteenth century who, in 1555, for the 'crime' of reading the English Bible, was arrested and charged with heresy. The Bishop of London tried in vain to persuade him to recant and, though still in his teens, he was sent to be burnt in his home town, as was then the custom. Pending his execution he was lodged at the *Swan*, Brentwood (Essex), an inn once known as the *Argent*, and later the *Gun*. The present *Swan* was rebuilt in 1931, but legend has it that Hunter's ghost still haunts the site of his last dreadful days on earth.

The *Parson & Clerk*, Streetly (Staffs), came by its name because of a feud between the local squire and the parish parson, the Reverend T. Lane. Squire John Gough, owned the inn, then known as the *Royal Oak*, but after a petty quarrel the parson used his influence to have its licence withdrawn. In retaliation Gough compelled the clergyman to hold a daily service by sending all his servants to form a congregation. Eventually the squire won and, in 1788, when he rebuilt the inn, he had two figures installed on the top. One was a parson, head lowered in prayer, and immediately behind stood a man with an axe uplifted as if to strike off the other's head. The figures have long since disappeared but the name of the inn, now a popular Ansell roadhouse, perpetuates the story.

The *Margaret Catchpole*, Ipswich (Suffolk) recalls the adventures of a woman who lived at the latter end of the eighteenth century. Born in Suffolk in 1773, she was the daughter of a labourer and the youngest of a family of six. Her first escapade occurred when she was thirteen and the wife of the farmer for whom she worked was taken ill. Margaret leapt on a huge dray horse and, without saddle or bridle, galloped to Ipswich to fetch a doctor. She later became a member of the household of an Ipswich brewery family, the Cobbolds, and was instrumental in saving one of the children from drowning.

Then, when she was twenty-four, she became infatuated with a ne'er-do-well and one day stole her master's horse to go and visit her lover. Dressed as a sailor, she rode from Ipswich to London, a distance of 70 miles in 8½ hours. She was arrested for theft, tried and sentenced to death, but thanks to the good impression she created at her trial and a special plea from her former employer, the sentence was commuted to seven years transportation. Within days she broke out of jail to join her lover, but was soon recaptured and sentenced to death for a second time. Again her fearless carriage in the dock won her much sympathy and the sentence this time was commuted to transportation for life. She arrived in Australia in 1801, married a respectable settler, and in due course they had a son and two daughters. When her husband died, he left her the bulk of his property. She moved to Sydney where, much respected, she died in 1841, aged 68.

In Ipswich museum today there are several letters and mementoes she sent from Australia. The son of her former benefactor, the Reverend Richard Cobbold, was given permission to write of incidents of her life, with the proviso that her husband's name was not revealed lest it harm the children. Published in three volumes in 1845, this story of her life has been reprinted many times, and though a number of fictitious incidents were added, no doubt is left as to her courage and indomitable will.

The Cobbolds are still brewers in Ipswich, and own the *Margaret Catchpole*. One side of the inn sign shows Margaret riding a horse a full gallop, and the reverse depicts a fictitious episode showing her with her lover fighting the coastguards.

Attached to the inn is a bowling green, and what more fitting than that the bowling club's badge should show the famous Margaret riding at full gallop?

In Swindon (Wilts) there is a nineteenth-century inn which was built as part of the village which the Great Western Railway Co laid out to house its employees in the early days of the railway works in the town. The origin of the inn's name, the *Glue Pot*, is unknown but there are two theories. The first that the workers used to take their glue pots with them to keep warm while they had a pint. The other, and perhaps more likely, theory is that the name came from the difficulty foremen had in getting their men back to work after the lunch break!

A word that is seldom used nowadays occurs in the name of an inn at Great Budworth (Cheshire). It is the *Spinner & Bergamot* and the name obviously dates from the period when Cheshire supported a busy weaving trade. For 'bergamot' is a woven cloth of flock and hair and was first produced in the Italian town of Bergamo, some 30 miles from Milan.

Tim Bobbin was the pseudonym of John Collier (1708–86) who achieved fame as the Lancashire dialect poet. Son of a poor country curate, he was born at Urmston, near Manchester, and was first apprenticed as a weaver at the age of fourteen. Later his indentures were cancelled and he became a roving schoolmaster. In 1729 he was appointed sub-master of a free school near Rochdale, where the total salary of the principal and himself amounted to only £20 a year. He acquired a knowledge of music, painting, modelling and etching, but his chief interest was in rhyming. He turned his hand, too, to carriage and sign painting, also to gravestone carving. He studied the Lancashire dialect and was an acute observer of character.

WHITBREAD

HOLFORD ARMS

WHITBREAD

NEVILL ARMS

NE VILE VELIS

WHITBREAD

ASGRE-LAN-DIOGEL-EI-PHERCHEN

IVOR ARMS

Bass Charrington

FORTE SCUTO SALUS DUCUM

Ebrington Arms

Bass Charrington

DEUS FORTIS ARCUS

Avon Inn

ASHBURTON ARMS

VIRTUS IN ARDUIS

FREE HOUSE

WHITBREAD

CAVENDISH

Bass Charrington

Shield & Dagger

WHITBREAD

HOWARD ARMS

Top (*l to r*): *Holford Arms,* Knockdown (Glos); *Nevill Arms,* Ashwood Bank, Redditch (Worcs);
Ivor Arms, Pontllanfraith (Mon)
Centre (*l to r*): *Ebrington Arms,* Ebrington (Glos); *Avon Inn,* Avonwick (Devon);
Ashburton Arms, West Charlton (Devon)
Bottom (*l to r*): *Cavendish; Shield & Dagger,* Southampton (Hants); *Howard Arms,* Ilmington (Glos)

In 1746, the first edition of his 'View of Lancashire Dialect', a humorous work, was published and was so popular that it was reprinted seven times during his lifetime. Continually reprinted since, it reached its sixty-fourth edition in the 1960s. Collier was buried in Rochdale churchyard.

That Lancashire still remembers its poet is evidenced by the two inns named after him, the *Tim Bobbin* at Rochdale, and another at Burnley.

Wiltshire people are known by the nickname of 'moonrakers', and the ridiculous story of its origin tells how some smugglers, finding themselves overlooked by coastguards, sank their contraband spirits in the river to be recovered later. When caught in the act of trying to retrieve the liquor by means of rakes, and asked what they were doing, the smugglers pointed to the reflection of the moon on the water and declared they were trying to rake out the cream cheese. Who could resist such a legend when looking for a name for an inn, and what better place than Swindon (Wiltshire) for the *Moonrakers*?

An inn which claims to be the oldest in Warwickshire was until recently called the *Old Green Man*, Bromford Lane, Erdington, Birmingham. It is an Ansell house and some beams dating back to AD 1300 were discovered when it underwent extensive alterations. It is said that the place was frequented by troopers during the Civil War and that there is a tunnel just outside the building which led to a nearby manor house. When the inn was re-styled the name no longer seemed appropriate, so it was renamed the *Lad in the Lane*, which was the nickname always given it by the 'locals'. Certainly there is no other inn of this name in Britain.

In the mid-nineteenth century, when the coaching era was in full swing, no coaching house was more popular at Henley-in-Arden (Warks) than the *White Swan*. Twenty-two coaches left Birmingham for London every day and seven of them called at the *White Swan*. The local court was held at the inn from 1845 to the early 1900s, when the police station was built.

But the inn had a history long before that for it was built about 1350 and much of the original structure survives. In the early years of the seventeenth century it was described as an inn with barn, stables, orchard and courtyard.

With the disappearance of the stage-coach the *White Swan* lost trade and there was a lean period but now Henley is again popular with tourists and the inn shares in the prosperity.

Coleshill, near Birmingham (Warks), was on the old stage-coach route and in those days the *Swan* was the most important inn, for it served as the stage for the Royal Mail on the London–Liverpool run.

There were, however, other attractions at Coleshill as Joseph Addison, the wit, essayist and poet, wrote in 1711. A horserace was run on Coleshill Heath for a six-guinea plate, and a plate of lesser value was awarded for a race between asses. At the same races, a gold ring was to be grinned for by men. The satirist, ending his piece, commented on the town dwellers' mystification at such simple rural pleasurers and went on:

. . . however it may be, I am informed that several asses are now kept in body clothes and sweated every morning on the heath and that all the country fellows within ten miles of the *Swan* grin an hour or two in their glasses every morning in order to qualify.

Typical of inns which carry a name for no apparent reason and without any local connection is the *Miller of Mansfield*, Goring (Oxon). It is the title of an old ballad which tells the story of Henry II losing his way and meeting a miller who, unaware of his importance, took him home to his cottage. Next morning courtiers came to find the king and the miller discovered the rank of his guest, who promptly dubbed him Sir John Cockle. Later Henry invited the miller, his wife and son to a royal banquet and made Sir John overseer of Sherwood Forest with a salary of £300 a year.

Any inn bearing the name *Passage House* is likely to be found close to the water and to have been built to serve those crossing a river or canal. Few, however, can claim to have been built on a Roman road and moreover, to have once been a guesthouse for bishops. This is but part of the history of the *Passage House* inn at the hamlet of Hackney, near Kingsteignton, a mile or so from Newton Abbot (Devon). The Roman road crossed the river Teign at Hackney and parts of mosaic pavements have been discovered at the inn. It is believed too, that bishops on their way to Torre Abbey used the building as a waiting place if the tide was not high enough for a crossing.

When other more convenient places were found to cross the river, the building became a farmhouse, but probably gained a new lease of life as an inn in 1790, when James Templer built the Stover canal to facilitate the transport of clay down to the river Teign. Later granite from Dartmoor, used to build the British Museum, London Bridge and other buildings of the metropolis, was floated down the canal to Teignmouth. The Hackney canal was built in 1843 to run from the river Teign to the Newton Abbot–Kingsteignton road and though only five furlongs in length it had a very useful life and survived until 1928.

Despite its convenient position for smuggling—it is 1½ miles down a narrow lane—the *Passage House* seems to have had unblemished character until a few years ago when customs men unsuccesfully searched the area on the lookout for a smugglers' ring which was believed to be using the rivers Teign and Dart as landing places. Today the farmhouse has been transformed into a delightful riverside inn and is a mecca for visitors.

For a long time the *Railway* inn, Cullompton (Devon) served a community within a community, for nearby are the winter quarters of a number of travelling showmen. Now the name has been changed to one which has found general favour, the *Showman,* and, to provide yet another link,

the inn overlooks a field which was the site of the town's annual fair for more than a century.

The new name was unveiled to the stirring sound of a 1908 Marenghi steam organ, mightily rendering 'Old Comrades', for the present landlord was formerly a professional musician and the bar is literally star-studded with photographs of famous people.

The colourful sign pictures a merry showman trying to convince an audience of the authenticity of a two-headed dwarf.

Bel and the Dragon, Cookham (Berks) is named after the legend which tells how Daniel convinced the king that Bel was only an image and not a living deity. A scene of this is on the sign.

Until the mid-fifties there stood in Hassett Street, Bedford, an inn known as the *Twist & Cheese.* It was purchased by Charles Well Ltd, the

Corner of a typical old English inn, the *Bear*, Bisley (Glos)

Bedford brewers, in 1897 but was demolished in 1955 to make way for planning improvements. At Lower Stondon (Beds) was the *Thatched House* under the same ownership. The name was a misnomer for the place had a slate roof, and it was a happy thought to take the name of the demolished premises for the inn that remained. Such an intriguing name must surely have a story attaching to it but, unfortunately, no one seems to know how the name came about.

The *Rutland Arms*, Newmarket (Suffolk), has been famous over 300 years for its association with the horse-races and bloodstock sales held in the town. Much of the present building can be dated back to the 1600s and it is reputed originally to have been part of the palace of Charles II. Nell Gwynne also had a house in nearby Palace Street and tunnels, since filled in, have been traced between the two. Many famous people associated with the turf have been visitors to the *Rutland Arms* and in one of the rooms there is still an outsize bed that was specially made for the late Aga Khan.

The ancient cobbled courtyard remains and, though much modernised, the inn still retains its attractive old world atmosphere.

There has been a *Bear* inn at Bisley village (Glos) in the Cotswold hills at least since 1639, for a copy of title deeds of that date is to be seen in the bar. The inn was then on the opposite side of the street, while the present inn was the court house and assembly room. Just why the court moved to the *Bear* is not clear, but that it did so is obvious from records showing that, in 1766:

> the Court of John Stevens was to be holden at the house of the widow Driver, known by the sign of the *Bear* inn in Bisley.

Apparently the court continued to meet at the inn until 1838.

Following the widow, John Hampstead, one of Nelson's captains, took over the place. In 1821 it was purchased by Joseph Watts, joint founder of a local brewery which had been formed in 1804, who remained the sole proprietor for the next fifty years. In 1888 the inn was purchased by the Stroud Brewery.

The inn retains many interesting features, including a fine seventeenth-century fireplace, complete with inglenooks and a jack. In the attic under the axe-hewn rafters is a huge oak pulley wheel, which probably had been used to turn the roasting jack in the kitchen.

Another inn, the origin of whose name is a complete mystery, is the *Drum & Monkey*, Stamford (Lincs). Existing records do not go beyond the mid-nineteenth century but the inn is certainly very much older than that. It was the *Sawyers Arms* a hundred years ago, then it became the *Slaters Arms*—in itself quite unusual—and after some years reverted back to the *Sawyers*. In 1950 it was re-named the *Drum & Monkey*, which is believed to have been the nickname by which it had long been known by the 'locals'. Some claim that the name arose after a travelling showman had halted outside the inn while his monkey performed a variety of tricks. Others believe that the name sprang in some way from the gypsies who used to gather nearby. Whatever the reason, the name is popular and has come to stay, illustrated by an attractive sign showing a monkey standing up and banging a drum.

Another intriguing name is the *Land o' Cakes*, Manchester (Lancs). It is from Burn's poem 'Peregrinations'.

A remarkable co-operative effort between the West Bromwich Corporation and Ansells Brewery has resulted in the preservation of a manor house, which has been described as a priceless example of a medieval timber-framed building.

Originally the property was purchased with demolition in mind, in order to form a small park, but closer examination of the building, which is believed to date back to *circa* 1290–1310, showed that it would be possible to repair and preserve it. The cost was met by the Corporation, assisted by grants from the Ministry of Works and the Pilgrim Trust.

The next problem was to find a suitable use for the building and finally Ansells Brewery put forward a scheme for licensed premises, which was accepted. So, after 600 years of occupation as a residence, the *Manor House*, West Bromwich, is now serving the community.

In its original state the house comprised a great hall, north solar wing, south-wing chapel, kitchen block and gatehouse, surrounded on all sides by a moat. All has been restored with the exception of the kitchen block which is a separate building.

It would be unthinkable for a house with such a history to be without its ghosts and the *Manor House* does not disappoint in this respect. A man with a black beard, and a little grey-haired old lady whose favourite occupation is peering through the windows, make their visitations, sometimes singly but occasionally together, and cleaners at work in the early morning have heard organ music.

The *Saye & Sele* in the village of Broughton (Oxon) takes its name from the family who reside in nearby Broughton Castle, the site of a manor house built in AD 1300. William of Wykeham, twice chancellor of the realm, purchased the manor in the fourteenth century and his son turned it into a fortified castle. Prior to the Civil War, prominent Cromwellians including John Pym, John Hampden and Lord Saye & Sele, met there in secret to lay their plans for the forthcoming struggle. In later, happier days, King Edward VII was a frequent visitor to the castle, often accompanied by 'Darling Daisy', Countess of Warwick.

The inn stands at the entrance to the castle grounds and carries as its sign the family coat of arms.

In the old days the painting of inn signs was a hit-and-miss affair. Sometimes itinerant artists would renew a faded sign for a meal and a drink, often with disastrous results. Today professional sign artists carry out considerable research before their work starts, and accuracy is the watchword.

When the *Black Dog*, Newent (Glos) was due for repainting, the artist borrowed Wing, a four-

The handsome black labrador, constant companion of Mr Michael Whitbread, was used as a model for the sign of the *Black Dog*, Newent (Glos)

year-old black labrador owned by Mr Michael Whitbread, a director of Whitbread Flowers Ltd, to be the model. The dog was taken down to the inn, where he was fully approved of by the 'locals' and proved himself a patient and intelligent 'sitter'. When the sign was unveiled, a newspaper headline announced: 'Director's dog goes on the board.'

The sign of the *Yorkshire Terrier*, a Whitbread house, Brinsworth (Yorks) was also modelled on a live dog, the pet of one of the brewery secretaries.

The sign of the *Haycock*, Wansford, near Peterborough (Northants), shows a farmer's boy floating down river on a haycock and is said to be based on a true story. Apparently a lad engaged in haymaking felt tired and lay down to sleep on a haycock close to the river. He slept so soundly that when the river flooded and took the haycock downstream, it carried the lad with it—much to his consternation when he did eventually wake up.

So badly had the fabric of the *Bull's Head*, Guildford (Surrey) deteriorated over the centuries that it hardly seemed worth renovating. Decay caused by death-watch beetles in the timbers had caused the walls to bulge and the ever increasing traffic on the high street had weakened the very foundations. Courageously, Whitbreads decided to restore the old inn, with the result that the present building, though completely modernised within, still presents the half-timbered Tudor exterior which has been so much a part of Guildford town since 1550. The name was originally the *Bull Head*, a name it retained for close on 300 years when it became the *Bull's Head*.

First mentioned in the parish registers in 1625, the inn is well documented and later records appear to indicate that the quartering of troops on innkeepers was not a paying proposition. A petition to Parliament from the inhabitants of the town in 1779 referred to the unhappy state of local innkeepers and supplied a list of thirteen 'people who have fail'd in Publik business in the three or four years last passed'. The list included William Crow of the *Bull Head*, and also Widow Coker of the *Bell*, who went bankrupt in 1773.

Yet the rental of the inn from 1780–99 was only £5 per annum, £6 in 1800, and £8 in 1829. True, that in the same fifty years taxes for the innkeeper rose from 14s 7d to £1 16s.

The sign of the *Hearts of Oak*, Drybrook, Forest of Dean (Glos), shows how heart-of-oak beams were selected from trees of chosen shape to build the old 'wooden walls', the ships of the English and later British Navy. Much of the oak which went into the ships was grown in the Forest of Dean and the New Forest (Hants). In Nelson's time, some 2,000 trees were required to build a seventy-four gun ship. His flagship HMS 'Victory' required 300,000 cubic feet of timber.

The *Hearts of Oak* sign also shows an Elizabethan warship of the type which defeated the Spanish Armada. The cross of St George supported by the royal cipher of Elizabeth and an oaken heart-shaped garland, completes this instructive sign. (Picture, p3.)

In Sheffield (Yorks) is the *Shiny Sheff*, a name which may puzzle some people but certainly not any of the complement of HMS 'Sheffield', a cruiser with an impressive battle record.

The inn's name was the cruiser's nickname, which it owed to the stainless steel deck fittings presented, among other gifts, by the City of Sheffield and of which the ship's company were exceedingly proud.

The cruiser's twelve battle honours (only two other Royal Navy ships out of the thousands at sea from 1939 to 1945 won a greater number) are displayed in the bar of the *Shiny Sheff*, together

with photographs and other mementoes of the cruiser.

Customers of Whitbread Wales' 430-year-old *Triangle* inn, Rhayader (Radnorshire), literally drop in for a game of darts—into a well cut in the floor. Since the taproom ceiling is only 6ft high, players have to step down into the well to give them sufficient headroom for throwing at the board. Licensee Mrs Garbett's 90-year-old mother herself held the licence of the *Triangle* for forty-nine years.

The *Queen's Larder*, situated in Queen's Square, London, WC1, had at one time an underground passage connecting it with a house nearby which was a residence of King George III. He is reputed to have lived there from time to time to be near the surgeons who were then treating him. The passage is now blocked off. The sign shows the Queen of Hearts about to place a tart in the larder, eagerly watched by the Knave.

Ian Lancaster Fleming was a man of many parts. Journalist, banker and stockbroker, he also served with British naval intelligence in World War II

A modern inn with an early aeroplane sign, Biggin Hill (Kent)

and was afterwards foreign manager of the 'Sunday Times'. He will, however, perhaps best be remembered as the writer of spy stories and creator of such famous characters as James Bond and Goldfinger. This is recalled by the name of a new inn, the *Goldfinger* Highworth (Wilts). The sign, which depicts the 'Goldfinger' character, was unveiled in 1972 by the author's widow who lived locally. (Picture, p31.)

The association between Lord Nelson and Lady Hamilton is recalled at the *Gun*, one of the famous inns by the river Thames at Deptford Reach, London. Here there is a circular staircase from which a door opens into a bedroom where the great admiral met his Emma.

Another Thames-side inn is the *City of Ramsgate*, Wapping, London, so-named because fishing boats from Ramsgate used to land their catches near the inn. Its claim to historical fame lies in the story that Judge Jeffreys, escaping from an enraged populace, rested at the inn pending the arrival of a boat which was to take him to France. Although disguised as a sailor he was recognised, arrested and sent to the Tower of London to save him from the mob. He died there soon afterwards. His hoard of 35,000 'guynies' and some silver was found on board the collier in which he had hoped to make his escape.

Near the Monument (City of London) which commemorates the great fire of London in 1666, is the *Monument*. The great column was erected by Sir Christopher Wren eleven years after the catastrophe. It stands 202ft high—the exact distance to the house in Pudding Lane where the fire originated.

In the same area are the *Old King's Head & Mermaid* and the *Cock* which enjoy special licensing hours to cater for workers in Billingsgate fish market.

In nearby Cannon Street there is the *London Stone*, standing close to the Stone, the oldest relic in the London streets and the milliarium from which the Romans measured all distances out of the city. Also in Cannon Street are the *Cannon* and the *Sugarloaf*, the latter a reminder that signs were also once used by tradesmen.

The *Flying Machine*, Biggin Hill (Kent), is a reminder of the nearby RAF fighter station which came into special prominence during the Battle of Britain in 1940. An unusual feature of the *Flying Machine* are the launderette machines on the premises, which are connected to a set of master lights in the bar to let each customer know when the wash has been completed.

High up on the Cheltenham–Northleach road (A40), which passes through the Cotswolds, is the *Puesdown*, whose picturesque two-sided sign reminds travellers just how bleak and savage the weather can be at this spot. It shows an early motorcar blocked by snowdrifts and the passengers endeavouring to push it clear. Tales are told of travellers being forced by deep snow to stay at the inn and on one occasion a hearse, complete with coffin and pall bearers, had an enforced stay of several days. The origin of the name goes back to Saxon times. (Picture, p45.)

Vauxhall gives its name to a station and a district of London, for in the seventeenth century the pleasure gardens there were a popular resort for Londoners. Pepys, the diarist, reported that the entertainments were 'mighty diverting'. The name emanated from Falkes, who was lord of the then manor. Strange, then, that the *Vauxhall* recalling all this is at Evesham (Worcs). The sign shows Londoners enjoying an entertainment in the gardens.

One of the most tragic yet ferocious campaigns that ever took place in England is recalled by an inn in the area of dykes, or 'bines' as they are locally known, at Western Zoyland, near Bridgwater (Som). It is the *Sedgemoor* and an attractive sign recalling the battle swings peacefully where nearly 300 years ago men's bodies swung from the gallows.

This, the last battle ever fought on English soil, was between the Protestant forces who had rallied to the banner of Monmouth, son of Charles II and his mistress, Lucy Walters, and the army of his uncle, King James II, who crushed the poorly armed and led rebels.

The retribution on the largely peasant army was severe. Judge Jeffreys made progress to the west and some hundreds were tried and transported for life. Monmouth was beheaded and over 200 of his supporters were also executed.

James' triumph did not last long. He fled the country and died in Rome in 1701. And in the course of time, by a queer twist of fate, Jeffreys was buried in a grave beside Monmouth in the Tower of London.

Long before there was an official racecourse at Cheltenham (Glos) horses were galloped across the fields in the vicinity. Fred Archer, the famous jockey who was born nearby, frequently rode there. In the early races visitors who flocked there used the Gotherington village inn as a vantage point

Some of the magnificent silver and enamel plaques which Asprey & Co of New Bond Street, London, have produced in a limited quantity as collector's pieces

that the name of the inn should now be the *Shutter*. (Picture, p39.)

When the marauding Vikings sailed up the Bristol Channel, they struck terror to the hearts of most people but not, so the story goes, to an old lady named Hobbs. She watched them beach their famous longships and when they moved off on the rampage, she calmly untied the boats and allowed them to drift downstream. This is recalled by the *Hobbs Boat*, Lympsham (Som). The colourful sign displays the boats with their red and white sails, complete with the insignia of the black raven.

The 'marcher' lords were appointed by William the Conqueror to maintain order in the marches or borders between England and Wales, and one of them was Robert Fitzhammon. In this capacity he was called in to suppress a local uprising near Barry (Glam) in 1091. His 3,000 men were divided between twelve of his knights, who each had an area to pacify, while he took the Margam area near what is now Port Talbot. The knights were paid for their services in gold, and a present-day reminder of this piece of history is the *Twelve Knights*, Margam. For good measure, a stretch of road nearby still retains its age-old-name, the Golden Mile.

By the upper wharf at Fareham (Hants) is the *Coal Exchange*, so-called because there was considerable coal trade done in the quarter. For some unknown reason, the area has always been known locally as 'Ickyboo'.

The *Black Rabbit*, Arundel (Sussex), is on the banks of the river Arun and was much used by the bargees on the Wey-Arun canal, opened in 1816 to facilitate the carriage of goods, particularly coal, from London to Arundel and Littlehampton. An unlucky canal in many ways, it went into liquidation in 1864 but there is now every likelihood that the waterway will be given a new lease of life as a tourist attraction.

Kent, too, has its smuggling inns and the *Star & Eagle*, Goudhurst, was once a haunt of the fraternity. From it there is a passage, still in existence, which led to the church next door to the inn. When the revenue men were hot on their trail, the smugglers immediately made for the tunnel and into the church, from which they could then emerge posing as respectable members of the community.

In 1972 the seventh Earl of Yarborough unveiled the sign of the *Pelham*, Immingham (Lincs), a Whitbreads East Pennines house. The Earl's ancestors fought at Poitiers in 1356, when 60,000 French were defeated by an English force of a quarter of that number. Sir John de Pelham played some part in the capture of the French king, an event which has been recorded in their coat of arms ever since by two silver buckled straps. The marriage of the fourth Earl of Yarborough and Marcia, Baroness Fauconberg, brought a shield of 153 quarters into the family. Much of this history is faithfully recorded on the family arms as the sign of the inn. The *Pelham* is near the present Earl's estate.

An inn at Glapwell, near Chesterfield (Derbyshire) rejoices in the unique name of *Young Vanish*. Few will know that it is named after a great racehorse which was famous from 1823 to 1832. Hearing the story from a member of the Houldsworth family who had owned the horse, Whitbreads felt that such a famous horse with local associations should be remembered. So the inn was renamed and the new sign bears a picture of the racehorse copied from a painting by the great animal painter, John F. Herring. Herring started life as a stagecoach driver and at one period drove the coach 'High Flyer' which ran between London and York. He later became a professional and very successful artist and painted portraits of thirty-three successive winners of the St Leger. (Picture, p83.)

The *White Horse*, Chilham (Kent), is undoubtedly an inn with a past, but unfortunately little of it has been recorded. Certainly it was in being in the fifteenth century, for an inglenook fireplace of that date was discovered a few years ago during alterations. Two male skeletons of unknown date were also unearthed and put to rest in the local churchyard. Today the inn stands in a quiet square with old beamed cottages and, despite the intrusion of the motor-car, retains its unruffled calm.

Another ancient inn at Pluckley (Kent) is the *Black Horse*, which is 560 years old. The village is said to be the most haunted in England, and certainly the old world atmosphere of the inn is in keeping with the belief.

PART II

Some Categories of Signs

RELIGIOUS SIGNS

From the earliest days of inns, when they were predominantly hostels set up for pilgrims by monasteries and abbeys, they naturally had signs of religious significance and through the centuries many of these have remained. They include:

Angel which, at Wetherby (Yorks), has a militant figure more like St George about to slaughter the dragon than an angel.

Church House is another name which survives. Most of the larger churches had their own brewhouses which later became inns. At Stoke Gabriel (Devon) one such has an excellent sign depicting medieval church builders with the implements of their trade. (Picture, p81.)

The *Royal Oak*, Meavy (Devon), was owned by the Church for centuries and in 1840 was given to the parish. Ever since, all profits have been used for the upkeep of the churchyard and other similar projects. Sometimes—as in 1973—the profits (£1,000) have been used to reduce the rates.

Crown, Capel (Surrey), a delightful rambling place, was formerly the vicarage and is almost next door to the church.

There are many *Anchor* inns, not necessarily situated in a port. Most of these sprang from 'Hope & Anchor', with hope as the anchor of the soul. The relevant verse may be found in Hebrews, ch 8, v 19. There is a *Hope & Anchor*, which originated in the fourteenth century, at Hope Cove, Kingsbridge (Devon).

The *Salutation* was also a popular name, and represented the angel saluting Our Lady. During the Civil War it was changed by the Puritans to the *Soldier & Citizen*.

The *Lamb & Flag* sign usually depicts the Holy Lamb with nimbus and banner.

The *St John*, Torpoint (Devon), has a sign of St John and the fish, and there is another *St John* opposite St John's church, Blackburn (Lancs). In London EC1, there is the *St John of Jerusalem*.

The *Good Samaritan* is at Ramsbottom (Lancs).

Jacob's Ladder is at Stratton (Wilts).

Noahs Ark is at Plymouth (Devon), with others

of the same name at Sheffield (Yorks) and St Albans (Herts).

Golden Cross is at Twyford (Berks).

Angel & Crown is at Highbury (London), and the sign shows an angel holding a crown.

There are several inns named *Adam & Eve*, including those at Paradise (Glos) and Newbury (Berks). Usually accepted as a religious sign, it is also derived from the arms of the Fruiterers Company, which was in existence in 1515.

ROYAL AND HERALDIC

Hundreds of inn signs bear the name or likeness of British monarchs from *Ethelbert*, king of Kent AD 560, Herne Bay (Kent), up to twentieth-century kings and queens. Where authentic portraits are available, sign artists usually model their signs on them, with pleasing results.

In Wulfstan Way, Cambridge (Cambs), is the *Queen Edith*, named after the wife of Edward the Confessor. She died in 1075, having made her mark by securing abolition of the custom which entitled bishops and abbots to receive kisses from the ladies.

There is a *Queen Bess* at Scunthorpe (Lincs).

Richard the Lion Heart is remembered as *Coeur de Lion*, Bath (Som).

The *King's Head*, Wateringbury (Kent), has a copy of the famous centuries-old window of the local church as its sign. It depicts Edward III and his queen, Phillippa.

There are hundreds of *Georges* in one form or another, but Henry VIII, Charles I, Charles II and Elizabeth I are the most numerous of the individual earlier monarchs to be featured on inn signs. In recent years Henry's ill-fated queens have increased in sign popularity. Ann Boleyn figures on a sign with the block and axe in the background at the *Queen's Head*, Box (Wilts) and Jane Seymour at the *Queen's Head*, Colney Heath (Herts), though she did not suffer the same fate as her predecessor.

A new heraldic sign is that of the *Rose & Portcullis*, Butleigh (Som) which pictures a portcullis on which is superimposed a Tudor rose.

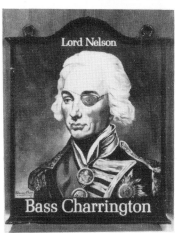

Top (*l to r*): *Virginia Ash*, Henstridge (Som); *Admiral Cunningham*, Fareham (Hants);
Duke of Beaufort, Hawkesbury Upton (Glos)
Centre (*l to r*): *Lord Nelson*, Ilminster (Som); *Waterloo House*, Bridgwater (Som); *Churchill*, West Lavington (Wilts)
Bottom (*l to r*): *Garrick's Head*, Cheltenham (Glos); *Duke of Monmouth*, Bridgwater (Som);
Pilot, Exmouth (Devon)

63

Charles II is usually pictured hiding from the Roundheads in a tree at scores of *Royal Oaks*, but at the *King Charles*, Bristol, the sign is a portrait of the monarch.

A portrait sign of Queen Anne at the *Queen's Head*, Neath (Glam), shows her as a young woman.

Both the Prince Regent and George IV, as he later became, are popular signs, but an original note is struck by *Prinny's*, Brighton (Sussex), which was the Regent's nickname. The inn has a Regency style decor.

The popularity of William IV, the sailor king, continues to live after him and he is remembered on several signs. A new *William IV*, Tunley (Som), has an excellent portrait and there is another at Shepton Mallet (Som). (Picture, p15.) At Rye (Sussex) there is a rare *Queen Adelaide*, his consort.

The poor old Duke of York who had 10,000 men is still popular and at Horfield (Glos) the sign of the *Duke of York* shows him with his soldiers and the hill on which he marched them up and down again.

There is a *Prince of Teck* in London, SW5.

Queen Victoria is a popular sign, and she is depicted at various ages, from child to widow, as at the *Queen*, Penzance (Cornwall). (Picture, p15.) Attractive too, is the penny black stamp at the *Queen's Head*, Lambeth, London, and in Bermondsey, London. At Great Titchfield Street, London, is a rare *Queen & Prince Albert*.

King George V is at High Wycombe (Bucks) and *Edward VII*, South Littleton (Worcs), Rushden (Northants) and Longlevens (Glos). (Picture, p15.)

Grave Maurice, Whitechapel Road, London, refers to Count Maurice of Nassau (1567–1625), afterwards Maurice, Prince of Orange, who made himself popular by opposing the Spanish domination of the Netherlands. Son of William the Silent, he waged a series of successful campaigns with English aid until Spain was finally compelled to acknowledge the United Provinces as a Free Republic.

Stoke-sub-Hamdon (Som) is a Duchy of Cornwall village, so it is fitting that the inn should bear the name of the *Duke of Cornwall*. The attractive signboard bears the portrait of Edward, the Black Prince, who was created the first Duke of Cornwall in 1337. The eldest son of Edward III, he led the van at the Battle of Crécy when only sixteen years of age and his nickname stems from black armour he wore at that battle. When he died in 1376 at the age of forty-six, he was buried with great pomp at Canterbury Cathedral, where his surcoat, helmet, shield and gauntlets are still preserved. On the sign of the *Black Prince* near Farnham (Surrey), he is shown as a resplendent mounted figure in surcoat and mail.

The royal arms are numerous all over the country and some of the signs are excellent reproductions of those of a particular reign. At the *King's Arms*, Stow-in-the-Wold (Glos) those of Henry VIII form the sign, while similarly named inns at Crewkerne (picture, p21) and Montacute (Som) display a modern version. It is often possible to obtain some idea of the age of an inn if, as is often the case, the original arms have been faithfully repainted from time to time.

FAMILY ARMS

Among the many services rendered by the inn sign by no means the least has been to record the associations of towns, villages and areas with local noble families. Each year sees further additions to this colourful category and some good new examples among hundreds are:

Anglesea Arms, Orpington (Kent)

Ashburton Arms, West Charlton, near Kingsbridge (Devon). (Picture, p53.)

Falkland Arms, Great Tew (Oxon)

Ilchester Arms, near Shepton Mallet (Som)

The *Howard Arms*, Ilmington (Glos), recalls that for centuries the Howards have been hereditary Earls Marshal of England. Their association with Ilmington began in 1843 when Henry Howard of Corby married the Canning heiress of nearby Foxcote. The sign commemorates the marriage. (Picture, p53.)

At Menai Bridge (Anglesey) is the *Bulkeley Arms*, named after a family of considerable note in the area. There was a Bulkeley, Bishop of Bangor, in the sixteenth century; a younger son of the family was Archbishop of Dublin in the seventeenth century and there was another, a Royalist general in the Civil War, who was later created a viscount. The inn, a Robinson house, bears the family coat of arms as its sign.

Most counties have an inn named after them, often with the coat of arms displayed. Unusual is the *Cornubia*, which is latinised 'Cornwall'. The arms are those of the Duke of Cornwall, whose father, Richard II, bore the title 'King of the Romans' in 1256.

POLITICIANS AND OTHERS

Not the least interesting signs are those commemorating comparatively unknown but nonetheless important personalities. It is due largely to such inn signs that we still know of their local associations, and many examples of this spring to mind.

The *Thomas Lord,* West Meon (Hants) honours a man (1755–1832) who achieved fame in two fields. He was a famous ornithologist and also a sportsman beloved of cricket enthusiasts as the founder of Lord's cricket ground. He retired to a farm at West Meon in 1830.

The *Duncombe Arms,* Hertford (Herts), commemorates a radical politician, Thomas Slingsby Duncombe (1796–1861), who first contested the Hertford division and was returned as its Member of Parliament in 1823. He took up the cause of imprisoned Chartists and foreign liberators, such as Mazzini and Louis Kossuth. There is a sign to the last named in North London.

In Wandsworth Road, London, is the *Lord Westbury,* named after a learned judge notorious for his sarcasm but who had no apparent connection with the district. Born Richard Bethell (1800–73) at Bradford-on-Avon (Wilts), he became Lord Chancellor with the title Baron Westbury of Westbury in 1861. A brilliant man and a zealous reformer, he carried through almost single-handed and against bitter opposition, a divorce and matrimonial Bill as early as 1857.

The sign at the *Lord Bexley,* Bexleyheath (Kent), shows the Bexley family's coat of arms. The first baron (1766–1851) was Chancellor of the Exchequer for twelve years during the Napoleonic Wars. He was created Baron Bexley in 1823.

John Bunyan (1628–88), born near Bedford (Beds), was the famous author of 'Pilgrim's Progress'. At Little Common (Herts) is the *John Bunyan.* The chimneystack of his cottage, which was nearby, is pictured on the sign.

The *Walpole,* Blackburn (Lancs), honours Sir Robert Walpole, first Earl of Orford (1676–1745), who became England's first prime minister. The story goes that when George I ascended the throne, he was reluctant to preside over meetings of his ministers because of his unfamiliarity with the English language and appointed Walpole in his stead. Walpole acquired the title in 1721 and retained the position for twenty-one years

There is a *Chandos* in the West End of London, obviously named after some member of the Brydges family. It could have been one of many as John, the first Baron Chandos, was enobled in 1554. He served Henry VIII well and suppressed the Wyatt rebellion. A later member of the family was a favourite of James I, and many others gave distinguished service to the country.

At Bath (Som) is *Byron House,* and its sign bears a portrait of the famous poet. In 1815, not far from the site of the inn, the poet's wife bought a large house and gave it to a Mary Carpenter who founded a reformatory school. Byron Place nearby was named after the poet.

At Middlesbrough (Yorks) is an inn named after the rebel who killed a collector of the poll tax and led a peasants' revolt. He presented demands to Richard II at Smithfield, London, in 1381. The *Wat Tyler* remembers him and his exploits.

A great seventeenth-century English playwright, John Fletcher (1579–1625), is remembered by the *Fletchers Arms,* Angmering-on-Sea (Sussex). Fletcher, the younger son of a Bishop of London, was born at Rye. He was a prolific writer and rates eight pages in the National Biographical Dictionary. He died of the plague.

The *Holford Arms,* Knockdown, Tetbury (Glos), honours Robert Stayner Holford, who founded and planned the very fine arboretum a few miles away at Westonbirt. He was the Squire of Westonbirt and began his collection in 1829. (Picture, p53.)

Happily, the tradition of naming inns after famous people is still being maintained, though on a smaller scale, and in 1971, the first inn to be named after Earl Attlee was opened. Called the *Clem Attlee,* it was built by Ind Coope Ltd at Fulham, London, and serves residents on Hammersmith Council's Clem Attlee housing estate. Earl Attlee knew the area well, having been born at Putney just across the river. Deputy prime minister under Churchill in 1942, he became prime minister of the first postwar government, 1945–51. Elevated to the peerage in 1955, he died in 1967.

It is still unusual for a man to be honoured by a sign in his lifetime, but the *Lord Stokes* has so complimented British Leyland's motor chief at Leyland (Lancs).

There are also hundreds of signs to lesser and even imaginary people:

Nell of Old Drury, Drury Lane, London, shows Nell Gwynne as an orange seller, reputed to be her occupation when she caught the eye of Charles II. There is also a *Nell Gwyne* in the Strand.

Eliza Doolittle is a new inn close to the Shaw theatre, Euston Road, London. The fictitious Eliza of Bernard Shaw's play 'Pygmalion', an instant success when it opened in 1939, achieved even greater fame in the musical play 'My Fair Lady' in 1956, followed by the film in 1964.

The *Cardinal,* Woking (Surrey) is so named after Cardinal Wolsey.

The *Lord Palmerston,* Highgate, London, commemorates the Liberal politician and prime minister (1784–1865)

Sir Joseph Paxton (1801–65) is remembered by the *Paxton's Head*, Finch House, Knightsbridge, London. He designed the Crystal Palace to house the international exhibition of 1851. Opened by Queen Victoria in 1854, the building was purchased by the Earl of Plymouth for the nation in 1911. It burnt down 1936. There is also a *Sir Joseph Paxton,* Titchfield (Hants).

Lady Godiva, Coventry (Warks), is a reminder of the legend first recorded in 1236. It tells of how the lady begged her husband to repeal certain taxes he had levied on the townspeople and of how he agreed to do so only on condition that she rode naked through the town. Lady Godiva did so, her husband kept his promise, and ever since 1678 the ride has been annually commemorated at Coventry.

In the village of Wickhamford (Worcs) is the *Sandys Arms*, its sign bearing the coat of arms of the famous family whose seat was once nearby. In the village church a pair of almost identical Jacobean tombs stand side by side: both are Sandys, and one of them became head of the family on the death of the other. It was a position he held for but a few hours before he, too, died.

The majority of 'Crown' inns represent traditional loyalty to the Crown, but some were so named because they stood on Crown lands. One such at Minchinhampton (Glos), the work of Stanley Chew, has a particularly attractive sign with the union under the Crown identified by the Cross of St George and the saltires of St Andrew, St Patrick and the red dragon of Wales. (Picture, p21.)

TRAVEL AND TRANSPORT
COACHING DAYS

Even in the eighteenth century the cities, particularly London, had a traffic problem which was contributed to in no small measure by the coaches which were then rapidly opening up the countryside.

From the *George and Blue Boar* inn, Holborn, London, no less than eighty-four coaches left every day going northwards, and from the *White Horse Cellar*, Piccadilly, some fifty coaches travelled daily to the west. A great number of London inns were also bases for other regular routes, such as the *Bull & Mouth*, St Martin's le Grand, which was a terminus for coaches running to the north-west. Another great coaching centre was the *Swan with Two Necks* and at its peak the owner of the inn himself had 1,800 horses and sixty-eight coaches on the road. Intense rivalry developed between the private companies (in which innkeepers often had

an interest) and indeed between them and the Royal Mail coaches. This competition so accelerated travelling time that, in their heyday, the 'crack' coaches were achieving on some long-distance runs an average of ten miles an hour.

The Royal Mail coaches were not given official names, though many of them acquired nicknames from an admiring travelling public, and in 1791, mail coaches on the main routes were covering $2\frac{1}{2}$ million miles a year. From London alone in 1835, twenty-eight Royal Mail coaches left nightly to carry mails to all parts of the country.

The coaches of the privately-owned companies all had names and some of these have come down to us thanks to the inns which were named after them. Two famous coaches were the 'Fly' and the 'Bull', both remembered by the *Flying Bull*, still at Rake (Hants). The *Glocester Flying Machine* has a fine reminiscent sign at Gloucester, as has the most famous of all the West Country coaches, the *Quicksilver Mail*, West Coker (Som). (Picture, p67.) One of the coaching inns near Falmouth (Cornwall) on this route was then known as *Indian Queens*. Today it is the name of the village itself.

The *Royal Blenheim* at Oxford; the *Eclipse*, Tunbridge Wells (Kent); the *Dairy Maid*, Aylesbury (Bucks); and the *Red Rover*, Barnes Common, London, all take their names from former coaches.

There are, also, many pleasing signs all over the country of the *Coach & Horses* (picture, p67), and a new and splendid sign to an old posting house is that of the *Old Coaching House*, Chudleigh (Devon). This, too, was the work of Mr Stanley Chew, a freelance artist responsible for many inn signs in various parts of the country. One of the largest—some 12ft wide by 6ft deep—at the *Coach & Horses*, Chislehampton (Oxon), was modelled on the replica in the Science Museum, London.

The coach trade gave employment to many hundreds of coachmen, guards, postboys, horsekeepers, horse-dealers, blacksmiths, harness-makers, wheelwrights and coachbuilders. The inns supplied postboys, ostlers and grooms, as well as their normal kitchen staff, chambermaids, porters, waiters and the like, and the whole business of coaching was run with the utmost efficiency and punctuality as competition became ever keener.

Hundreds of other names and signs survive from the coaching and horse era, including the *Royal Mail, Postboy, Horse & Groom, Farriers, Toll Gate, Three Horseshoes, Four Horseshoes* and even *Five Horseshoes, Turnpike, Horse & Cart,* Peasmarsh (Sussex) and *Wait for the Waggon*, Wyboston (Beds). Among others are the *Stable Door,*

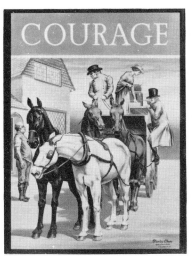

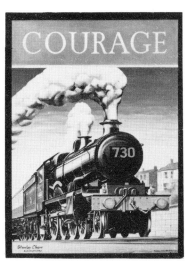

Top (*l to r*): *Travellers Rest*, Staxton (Som); *Coach & Horses*, Clifton, Bristol; *Quicksilver Mail*, West Coker (Som)
Centre (*l to r*): *Terminus*, Cardiff (Glam); *Locomotive*, Newton Abbot (Devon); *The Bridge*, Yatton (Som)
Bottom (*l to r*): *Iron Horse*, Wroughton (Wilts); *Great Western*, Yeovil (Som); *Silent Whistle*, Oakle Street (Glos)

OLD COACHING HOUSE

The unexpected hazards and liveliness of the coaching era is captured on
this sign at Chudleigh (Devon)

Mailcart, Spalding (Lincs) and the *Carters Rest*, Wroughton (Wilts). There is an excellent *Van & Horses*, Uxbridge (Middx) and a cut-out old style waggon at the inn of that name at Belsay (Northumberland).

The *Tradesmen's Arms*, Stokenham (Devon), was once a stopping point for packhorses and drivers on the route from Dartmouth to Kingsbridge.

THE RAILWAYS

There were some 3,000 coaches on the road employing 150,000 horses when, in 1825 the opening of the first railway—Stockton to Darlington—for passenger and general traffic marked the beginning of the end of coaching, although many private coach services were to struggle on for another twenty-five years.

Considering the time it had taken to make use of the coaches for carrying mails, the Post Office was quick to avail itself of the 'new-fangled' railways. The Liverpool & Manchester Railway was opened in September 1830 and two months later it carried its first royal mail consignment. By 1844, royal mail trains were averaging 27mph and the only reminder of the coaching era was the Post Office guard who rode on a perch near the carriage roof.

Many of the inns close to the new railway stations hastened to change their names to attract railway custom, and almost overnight they became the *Railway* or *Locomotive* inn or arms, the *Great Western, South Eastern, Great Northern*, according to the line which served their area. There is still a *Railway Terminus*, Bridport (Dorset) and a *Railway Telegraph*, Forest Hill, London.

Now that the age of steam has come to an end, nostalgia and sentiment are finding expression in new inn names and signs with railway associations. Some particularly fine signs depict the 'crack' engines of the past. The sign of the *Puffing Billy* at Blandford Forum (Dorset), shows an engine of *circa* 1813; the *Engine,* Newcastle upon Tyne (Northumberland) pictures the 'Rocket'; the *Marlow,* Marlow (Bucks) has a donkey engine, while a 'North Star', an 1837 type of engine, is on the sign of the *Great Western,* Warwick, and also on the sign of the *Steam Engine,* Lambeth, London, near the former GWR South Lambeth depot. The *North Western,* New Mills, near Stockport (Cheshire) and *North London,* Camden Road, London, have signs showing a North London train.

Famous engines of a later period can be identified on such inn signs as those of the *Silver Bullet* (the LNER streamlined train) at Finsbury Park, London, and the *Royal Scot,* Carlisle (Cumberland).

There is a *Railway Signal,* London, SE23; a *Chatham & Dover Railway,* London, SW11, while the *South Eastern* at Tonbridge (Kent) recalls the railway company of that name. Folkestone (Kent) has the *Golden Arrow,* and there is an *Engine & Tender* at St Neots (Hunts).

Following the railway closures of 1963 and 1965, a number of inns which were affected were renamed as, for instance, the *Silent Whistle,* Evercreech (Som). Another *Silent Whistle* is at Oakle Street (Glos). (Picture, p67.) Formerly the *Oakle Street* inn, alongside the station, it, also changed its name when the Beeching axe fell.

The *Railway,* Hornchurch (Essex) has on its sign an electric multiple unit and on the reverse a Great Eastern steam train. Similar signs are to be found at Pitsea and West Horndon (Essex), which is strange, as these areas were not served by the Great Eastern but by the London, Tilbury & Southend Railway.

Almost every form of transport has found its way on to inn signs, as evidenced by this far from comprehensive selection:

Silver Ghost, Alvaston (Derbyshire) with a sign showing a Rolls Royce on one side and a ghost on the other

Fire Engine, Bristol

Traveller's Rest, Grasmere (Cumberland) with a sign depicting a penny-farthing bicycle

Tramcar, Sheffield (Yorks)

Tramway, Colchester (Essex)

Old Tramway, Stratford-on-Avon (Warks) shows on its sign an early type of horse-tram

Bicycle, Rotherfield (Sussex)

Victoria, Esher (Surrey), with a sign picturing the four-wheeled carriage of that name

Milecastle, near Haltwhistle (Northumberland), which stands near Hadrian's Wall, has a full-size replica of a Roman chariot outside the premises. The inn takes its name from the mile castle of the

Roman fortifications that stood on the wall close by

Metropolitan, Uxbridge (Middx) shows an A60 tube train on its sign.

AIR TRAVEL

A very early attempt at flight is recorded on the sign of the *Flying Monk,* Malmesbury (Wilts) where a monk fell from the abbey tower in an unsuccessful attempt to fly with the aid of artificial wings.

Ballooning was also a popular subject for innkeepers in its early pioneering days, and there is still at least one such sign, the *Air Balloon,* Brockworth (Glos).

Several inns are named after aircraft that were built locally, as, for instance, the *Wayfarer,* Bristol; *Canopus,* Rochester (Kent); *Harrier,* Hamble (Hants); *Britannia,* Hackney, London. Many aircraft which became famous in the 1939–45 war have also received the inn sign accolade, as at the *Flying Lancaster,* Desford (Leics). At Knowle, near Bristol, is *Happy Landings,* the sign of which shows a helicopter landing.

SHIPS

As an island race, the people of Britain take particularly kindly to signs dealing with the sea and ships. The following are a selection:

Sea Around Us, Loughborough (Leics)

Square Rigger, City of London

The *Ship,* West Croydon (Surrey) has an attractive white ship's figurehead as a sign

Frigate, St Martins Lane, London

City Barge, Chiswick, London

Hoy, Greenwich, London

Steamer, Preston (Lancs)

Severn Trow, Stourport (Worcs). These boats, made at Stourport, carried goods from Stafford and Worcestershire down to Bristol

Cape Horner, Swansea (Glam)

Pilot Boat is fairly common in river and sea ports

The *Ship,* Caerleon, (Mon) has a sign showing a Roman galley of the type which travelled up and down the river to the legionary fort at Caerleon-on-Usk. (Picture, p49.)

And where better for *Old Father Thames,* than near London's river at Lambeth?

SPACE TRAVEL

Quite a few signs of the space-age have appeared in recent years, and the *Flying Saucer,* Gillingham (Kent), was one of the earliest. Others include

Other Side of the Moon, Nottingham (Notts); *Telstar*, Stockton (Co Durham); *Satellite*, Liverpool; *Man in Space*, Stoke-on-Trent (Staffs); and *Half Moon*, Milford (Surrey), the sign of which pictures a moon rocket. There was *Man in the Moon*, Birmingham, but after the success of the first landing, the inn, with commendable speed, was renamed *Man on the Moon*.

NAVAL AND MILITARY

In addition to signs depicting military and naval subjects, a whole host of famous, or just popular soldiers or sailors are represented in the signboard gallery.

Lord Nelson, hero of Trafalgar, easily leads and there are few towns in the country that do not boast a *Nelson*, prefixed by either 'Admiral' or 'Lord'. Others show his likeness on the board but the name of the inn is *Hero*. Mostly the portraits are excellent likenesses, taken from contemporary portraits. *Lord Nelson*, Norton-sub-Hamdon (Som) is a new one and, fittingly, there is also one at Dartmouth (Devon), home of the Royal Naval College.

There are, too, hundreds of inns named after the Duke of Wellington. They come in various styles, *Hero of Waterloo*, *Duke of Wellington*, *Iron Duke*, etc, but there is only one which descends to the vernacular, that is the *Dook*, Falmouth (Cornwall), with the famous soldier depicted on its sign. *Waterloo House*, Bridgwater (Som), has a sign showing the duke with cannon and drum in the foreground. (Picture, p63.) At Waterloo, near Taddington (Derbyshire), a very fine sign depicts British troops forming a hollow square, a defensive tactic which proved so successful at the battle. The inn is the *Waterloo*, and a similar scene is pictured on the sign of the *British Flag*, Gloucester (Glos).

A monument to the duke crowns a hill at Wellington (Som), the town from which he took his title, so it is fitting that there is a *Wellington Arms* at Rorks Bridge (Som), nearby.

Among other popular names in this category is that of the Marquis of Cornwallis (1738–1805). Born in London, he followed a military career and was ADC to the Marquis of Granby, another famous soldier who has had many inns named after him. Cornwallis fought in the American War of Independence and in 1790 was commander-in-chief of the army which fought Tippoo Sahib of Mysore. As governor-general of India (1786) he carried out many reforms, and is now remembered by the *Marquis of Cornwallis*, Bethnal Green, London.

James Wolfe was born in 1727 in the vicarage at Westerham (Kent). After a colourful military career he died, aged thirty-two, on the Plains of Abraham after defeating the French at Quebec. He is remembered in the village of his birth by the *General Wolfe*, which has a colourful two-sided sign.

The *Marquis*, Rhosybol (Anglesey) a Robinson house, commemorates the Marquis of Anglesey, who was second-in-command at the Battle of Waterloo. Close by the Menai bridge is a 250ft column surmounted by a statue, which was erected to the memory of this popular soldier, after whom many other inns in various parts of the country are named.

At Uxbridge (Middx) is the *Lord Hill*, a reminder of the first Baron Hill (1772–1842), a distinguished soldier who was the Duke of Wellington's right-hand man at Waterloo. Though suffering from severe wounds, he was responsible for sweeping Napoleon's 'Old Guard' from the field, and when Wellington became prime minister, he succeeded him as commander-in-chief of the army, a post he held for fourteen years.

Admiral Robert Blake (1599–1657), the eldest of twelve sons, was born in Bridgwater (Som), where he attended the local grammar school. When the Civil War loomed, he joined the Parliamentary army and rose to become one of Cromwell's generals at sea, where he fought brilliantly against the Dutch and Spaniards. On his death, he was given a state funeral and buried in Westminster Abbey, but at the Restoration his body was removed and cast into a pit dug on the north side of the abbey. His last resting place is, therefore, unknown but in his native town of Bridgwater a statue and the *Blake Arms* inn, with its sign, ensure that he is not forgotten.

As a boy of fourteen, John Franklin (1786–1847) entered the navy and took part in the battles of Copenhagen and Trafalgar. Later he made extensive explorations along the Arctic coast of Canada, and in 1845 led the expedition which discovered the north-west passage. Knighted in 1829, he became governor of Van Dieman's land (Tasmania). At Poplar, London, there is now the *Sir John Franklin*.

There are several inns named after *General Gordon* (1833–85), including one at Nelson (Lancs).

Lord Roberts (1832–1914) was at the siege of Delhi and later played a prominent part in the suppression of the Indian mutiny and the relief of Lucknow. A major-general in the Afghan War (1878), he subsequently became commander-in-chief, India, led a British force in the Boer War,

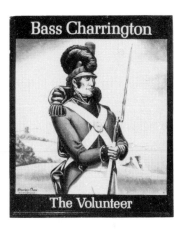

Top (*l to r*): *Volunteer*, Seavington (Som); *British Flag*, Bridgwater (Som); *Yeoman*, Gloucester (Glos)
Centre (*l to r*): *Centurion*, Lincoln (Lincs); *Royal Yeoman*, Grimstone (Dorset); *Volunteer*, Lyme Regis (Devon)
Bottom (*l to r*): *Gordon Arms*, Fareham (Hants); *Hearts of Oak*, Barnstaple (Devon);
Royal Artillery Arms, West Huntspill (Som)

and was promoted to field marshal on his elevation to the peerage in 1892. He died while visiting troops in France in 1914, and the inn which now bears his name is the *Lord Roberts*, Sandy (Beds).

REGIMENTAL SIGNS

The many signs recalling the history and traditions of British regiments and naval units are particularly to be treasured today, when so many are losing their identity through disbandment or amalgamation.

Among these is the splendid two-sided sign which adorns the *Royal Gloucestershire Hussar*, Frocester (Glos). On one side is a mounted hussar in the dress of a colonel of the regiment at the turn of the century and, on the reverse, the badge and battle honours of the regiment. The sign is the work of John Cook, the chief artist of Whitbreads. Once the *George*, the name of the inn was changed in 1968 to honour the county's territorial regiment. Regimental silver, souvenirs and dummies in full dress are to be seen in the bars.

A new inn sign adorns the *Cannon*, Ash, near Aldershot (Hants). It depicts a cannon in the possession of F (Sphinx) Parachute Battery, RHA, which was abandoned during the withdrawal from the North-West Frontier in 1841 and recovered forty years later from an enemy fort after the Battle of Ahmed Khel.

The *Buckinghamshire Yeoman*, Aylesbury (Bucks), was opened in 1969. The name was chosen to commemorate the famous local regiment and the sign shows a mounted Bucks hussar. Among the mementoes in the inn associated with the regiment is a drawing of one of the last cavalry charges of the British army, made by the Royal Bucks Hussars in Palestine in 1917. A local, still alive, who is featured in the drawing was then a bugler boy and was awarded the Military Medal for his part in the action.

The Queens Own Dorsetshire Yeomanry was founded in 1881, an event recorded on the fine sign of the *Royal Yeoman*, Grimstone (Dorset), with its painting of a cavalryman. Also in Dorset, near Dorchester, is the *Trumpet Major*, whose figure adorns the sign.

Other signs with military or regimental associations include: the *Royal Artillery Arms*, West Huntspill (Som) (Picture, p71); the *Trooper*,

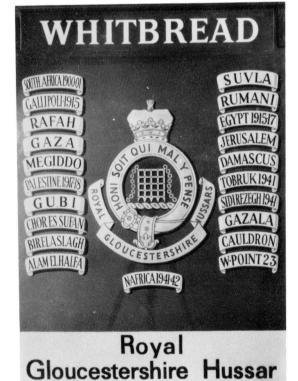

An excellent example of a sign which is both picturesque and informative.
Two-sided, the sign is at Frocester (Glos)

Plaisterer's Arms, Winchcombe
(Glos)

Baker's Arms, Chipping Camden
(Glos)

Blacksmiths Arms, Plymtree
(Devon)

Carpenter's Arms, Dundry
(Som)

Brickmakers Arms, Barons Cross,
Leominster (Herefs)

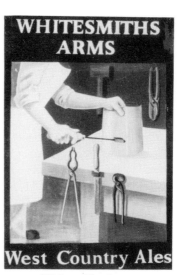

Whitesmiths Arms,
Gloucester (Glos)

73

Windsor (Berks); and the *Drill*, Gidea Park (Essex), with its sign of a sergeant-major on the parade ground.

The *Volunteer*, Seavington (Som), has a two-sided sign showing volunteers in uniforms worn for two threatened invasions, those of Napoleon and Hitler, while another of the same name at Lyme Regis (Dorset), has a sign featuring one of the Sherborne Volunteers of 1804. (Picture, p71.)

Then there is the *Horse Guards*, Tillington, Petworth (Sussex); the *Imperial Forces*, Chatham (Kent); the *Forces*, Dittisham (Devon); and the *Gordon Arms*, Fareham (Hants), the sign shows a Gordon Highlanders' piper. (Picture, p71.)

The *Ark Royal*, Plymouth (Devon), has a splendid two-sided sign of the aircraft-carrier of that name, while an old-time ship-of-the-line dominates the sign of the *Ship's Tavern & King's Head*, Plymouth (Devon). Originally the *King's Head*, it acquired its second name on enlargement and there is a portrait of Charles I in one corner of the sign. (Picture, p49.)

Many land and sea battles are remembered by inns and their signs, especially those of the Crimean War. There is a *Crimea*, Castleford (Yorks), *Balaclava*, Blackburn (Lancs), and several named *Alma*, *Inkerman*, *Sebastapol*. There is a *Zulu*, Ipswich (Suffolk), as well as a *Malta*, *Gibraltar Castle*, *Cyprus*, *Cuba*, *Odessa* and many more. The *Senlac*, Battle (Sussex), is named after the hill on which the famous battle was fought in 1066. The *Desert Rat*, remembering the 8th Army of the World War II, is at Reigate (Surrey).

TRADES AND CALLINGS

One of the few remaining reminders of the time when most tradesmen's premises were identified by a distinctive sign is the barber's pole. In the days when they were barber/surgeons, the bloodied bandage round the pole was instantly recognised. Later, pharmacists adopted the pestle and mortar and, later still, the coloured carboys. Another trade sign was the three sugarloaves of the grocer, and there are four inns called the *Three Sugarloaves*, at Hedingham (Essex); Luton (Beds); Croydon (Surrey), and Hollingbourne (Kent).

At one time almost every trade or guild of craftsmen was represented on an inn sign, and even if some had no recognised badge or coat of arms the name itself served to advertise the headquarters of that particular group. Many of these old inn names still survive to remind us of trades and callings which have long since disappeared. Among them are the following and in most cases they are either prefixed with the word 'Jolly' or have 'Arms as a suffix.

Plaisterers, Winchcombe (Glos). (Picture, p73.)

Brushmakers, Upham (Hants)

Carpenters, Dundry (near Bristol). The sign shows a bandsaw, adze and plane. (Picture, p73.)

Chairmakers, Worlds End (Hants)

Trowel & Hammer, Marks Tey (Essex)

Jolly Collier, Radstock (Som), where coalmines are still worked

Jolly Coopers, Flitton (Beds)

Colliers, Radcliffe, near Manchester (Lancs)

Three Jolly Colliers, London, SE1

Sawyers, Rochdale (Lancs)

Hatters, Marple, near Stockport (Cheshire)

Treble Tile, West Bergholt (Essex)

Whitesmiths. These were men who worked with 'white' metals as distinct from blacksmiths. There is a *Whitesmiths*, Gloucester (Glos) and another at Wigan (Lancs). (Picture, p73.)

Spindlemakers, Preston (Lancs)

Gardeners, Whalley Range, Blackburn (Lancs)

Printers, Blackburn (Lancs)

Quarryman's, Blackburn (Lancs)

Waggonmakers, Bury (Lancs)

Engineers, Henlow (Beds)

Millers, Singleton, near Blackpool (Lancs)

Ye Olde Pipemakers, Rye (Sussex)

Shoe, Exton (Hants), with a coloured sign showing an old-fashioned shoe

Gamekeeper, Compton Dando (Som). (Picture, p75.)

Spinners, Darwen (Lancs)

Stonemasons, Heywood (Lancs)

Turners, Blackburn (Lancs)

Traders, Mellor, near Blackburn (Lancs)

Hand & Shuttle, Padiham (Lancs)

Snuff Mill, near Bristol

Jolly Weavers, Banbury (Oxon)

Merchants, Bristol and Blackburn (Lancs)

Chalk Drawers, Olney Heath (Bucks), with a modern sign showing men loading chalk

Chainmakers, Cradley Heath (Worcs) and Walsall (Staffs)

Glassmakers, Bromsgrove (Worcs)

Nailors, Bromsgrove (Worcs)

Brick & Tile, Eight Ash Green (Essex)

Auctioneers, Measham, near Ashby-de-la-Zouch (Leics)

Coopers, Ashton, Bristol

Yarnspinners, Spondon (Derbys)

Woodmans, Halstead (Essex); Newcastle upon Tyne (Northumberland), and at Black Fen (Kent), where the sign shows a woodman at work on a pedestal 12ft high

THE HOP POLE

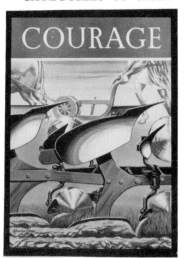

The Bull

Plough

Gamekeeper Inn

Bass Charrington

Red Cow

Top (*l to r*): *Farmers Arms*, St Brides Major (Glam); *Hop Pole*, Cheltenham (Glos); *Plough*, Thornbury (Glos)
Centre (*l to r*): *Harvesters*, Galhampton (Som); *The Bull*; *The Plough*, Cold Ashton (Glos)
Bottom (*l to r*): *Gamekeeper*, Compton Dando (Som); *Waggon & Horses*, Glastonbury (Som);
Red Cow, Honiton (Devon)

75

Bowlturners, Leicester (Leics)

Tinners, Zennor (Cornwall), also at Blackburn (Lancs). There is a *Tin Mans* in the Forest of Dean (Glos)

Thatchers, Great Warley (Essex)

Stokers, Blackburn (Lancs)

Tanners, near Blackburn (Lancs) and Horsham (Sussex)

In addition to inns named after specific trades, there are also many which bear names associated with a trade, as for example:

Bettell & Chisel, Delabole (Cornwall), 'bettell' being the old name for a mallet

Flying Shuttle, Farnworth (Lancs)

Hand & Shuttle, Padiham (Lancs)

Knife & Cleaver, Houghton Conquest (Beds)

Miners Rest, Chasetown (Staffs)

Baker & Oven, Twickenham (Middx)

Pig of Lead, Cromford (Derbyshire), also at Bonsall (Derbyshire). Lead was mined in this area from Roman times

Three Furnaces, Warley (Lancs)

Open Hearth, Scunthorpe (Lincs). The sigh shows a steel furnace on one side and an open fire in a hearth on the other

Anvil, Warley (Lancs)

Hammer & Pincers, Wymeswold (Leics)

Locomotive, Ashford (Kent) where many railway engines were once built

Shepherdess, City Road, London, where sheep roamed less than 300 years ago

Lobster Smack, Canvey Island (Essex)

Trawler, Brixham (Devon)

Brickmakers. There is a new one of this name at Barons Cross, Leominster (Herefordshire) with a sign showing the authentic brickmakers' arms. (Picture, p73.)

Some inns have names associated with their own trade, and from earliest days there have been a number called *Grapes* or *Vine*. Other fairly common ones are: *Malt Scoop*, *Jolly Brewer*, *Three Tuns* and the more unusual *Leather Bottell*, Lewknor (Oxon), *Leathern Bottel*, Cranfield (Beds) and Wavendon (Bucks) and *Half Butt*, Gt Horkesley (Essex).

AGRICULTURAL AND COUNTRYSIDE

Agriculture, horticulture and trees all have their share of inn signs, some of them very attractive:

Walnut Tree, Ditton (Kent). Commemorates a nearby tree of prodigious size which provided many of the nobility and gentry of Kent with gunstocks.

Another, at Pyle (Glam) shows a tree, walnuts and a gunstock

Walnut Tree, Matfield (Kent), has a sign representing the old rhyme: 'A woman, a dog and a walnut tree, the more you beat them the better they be'

Plough, Thornbury (Yorks). The sign depicts a Roman wooden plough drawn by an ox, and a modern reversible plough (Picture, p75))

Plough, Cold Ashton (Glos) has a very fine sign showing a horse-drawn plough (Picture, p75)

Butter Churn, Carshalton (Surrey)

Flower Pot, Remenham (Berks)

Mulberry Bush, Kempston (Beds)

Crab Tree, Adlyfield, Hemel Hempstead (Herts)

Farmers Arms, St Bride Major (Glam) (Picture, p75)

Harvesters, Galhampton (Som) (Picture, p75)

Flowers of the Forest, Blackfriars Road, London, SE1, whose sign is a delightful painting of wild flowers

Swingletree, Callington (Cornwall), named after the crossbar to which a horse's traces are attached

Surrey Oaks, Newdigate (Surrey)

Sheaf & Sickle, Rugby (Warks) and elsewhere

Jolly Thresher, Lymm (Cheshire)

Yellow Rose, Middlesbrough (Yorks)

Blossoms, Chester (Cheshire)

Tulip Tree, Richmond (Surrey), and others

Honeypot, Queensbury, N London

Orange Tree, Hitchin (Herts) and Totteridge (Herts)

Oak & Acorn, Rosebarton (Som)

Pineapple, Dorney (Bucks). Said to have been where the first pineapple was grown in England, though the name is not uncommon for an inn. There is another at Marple (Cheshire)

ANIMALS, BIRDS, FISH AND REPTILES

Almost every animal from whales to elephants and kangaroos appears on inn signs. Here are a few inns which feature their namesake on their sign:

Cow & Calf, Romiley, near Stockport (Cheshire)

Dog & Partridge, near Stockport (Cheshire)

Green Dragon, Combe St Nicholas (Som) (Picture, p78); Hardraw (Yorks) and Kirkby Lonsdale (Westmorland)

Red Dragon, Kirkby Lonsdale (Westmorland)

Dolphin, Ilminster (Som) (Picture, p78)

Grey Mare, Oswaldtwistle (Lancs)

Full Moon, Stokes Croft, Bristol, with a howling wolf as its sign (Picture, p78)

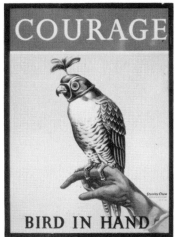

Top (*l to r*): **The Cock**, Warminster (Wilts); *Flying Swan*, Hookagate (Salop); *Full Moon*, Bedminster, Bristol
Centre (*l to r*): *Falcon*, Fawley (Hants); *Gamecock*, Cheltenham (Glos); *Cranford*, Exmouth (Devon)
Bottom (*l to r*): *Milford*, Yeovil (Som); *Tern*, Yate (Glos); *Bird in Hand*, North Curry (Som)

White Horse

WHITE HART

Lamb

Beehive

Dolphin

Top (*l to r*): *White Horse*, Wallington (Hants); *White Hart*, Cinderford (Glos); *Lamb*, Great Rissington (Glos)
Centre (*l to r*): *Black Horse*, Bristol; *Beehive*, Yeovil (Som); *Full Moon*, Stokes Croft, Bristol
Bottom (*l to r*): *Green Dragon*, Combe St Nicholas (Som); *Dolphin*, Ilminster (Som);
Fox & Hounds, St Brides Major (Glam)

Little Pig, Bromsgrove (Worcs)

White Hart, Yetminster (Dorset)

Lions and horses appear with strange companions and in a variety of colours and postures on signs all over the country. The lion may be black, white, red, yellow, brown, golden or even green, as at Rochester (Kent). There is even a silver lion mounted on a pedestal 10ft high at Lilley, near Hitchen (Herts). At Godalming (Surrey) is a *Three Lions*, and at Plaistow (Essex) a *Black Lion*.

Brown Bear, Devonport (Devon), has a wallplate 6ft high as its sign

Bull (Picture, p75)

Bulldog, Waltham Cross (Herts)

Dog & Badger, Clophill (Beds)

Dog & Badger, Medmenham (Bucks)

Dog in a Doublet, Crowland (Lincs)

Elephant's Head, Hackney, London

Fallow Buck, Enfield (Middx)

Garland Ox, Bodmin (Cornwall)

Jackal, Thurleigh (Beds)

Kicking Cuddy, Bowlees (Durham), deriving from the local name for a horse

Kicking Donkey, Burwash (Sussex) and Dunmow (Essex)

Leopard's Head, Blackburn (Lancs)

Mole, Monks Sherborne (Hants). Sign shows a delightful little fellow lying back replete after a meal

Molescroft, near Hull (Yorks). Here the mole is shown digging

Pit Ponies, Easton, Bristol

Polar Bear, London, WC2

Seahorse, Gosport (Hants), Porthcawl (Glam) and York (Yorks)

Spotted Dog, Smarts End, Penshurst (Kent)

Stag's Head, Hinton Charterhouse (Som)

White Boar, Bury (Lancs)

Horses, too, are numerous and generally represent a particular breed, such as the *Suffolk Punch*, Ipswich (Suffolk), and again at Boreham Wood (Herts). There is a *Cleveland Bay*, Redcar (Yorks) while a fine new sign at the *Red Cow*, Honiton (Devon), shows a specimen of the local breed (Picture, p75).

Dogs and cats, as would be expected, are equally numerous and include:

Romping Cat, Bloxwich (Staffs)

Burmese Cat, Melton Mowbray (Leics)

Cat and Custard Pot, Shipton Moyne (Wilts) (Picture, p89)

Cat's Whisker, Childwall (Lancs)

It is said that the first Labrador dog ever brought into Britain was owned by a Weymouth (Dorset) licensee, and that it was he who named his inn

the *Black Dog*. At this ancient inn Daniel Defoe, who wrote 'Robinson Crusoe', once stayed.

Still more animals after which inns are named are:

Bull & Tiger, Boreham Wood (Herts)

Bear, Devizes (Wilts), with an unusual sign showing the animal with a bunch of grapes in its mouth

Badger & Box, Annesley (Notts)

Panther, Reigate (Surrey)

Zebra, Cambridge (Cambs)

Birds of all kinds, from the humble sparrow to an ostrich have always been popular inn names. Examples are:

Black Robin, Kingston (Surrey)

Black Swan, Langport (Som)

Bullfinch. As one of Britain's most colourful native birds, this is particularly popular and the subject of a handsome new sign at Innsworth (Glos)

Cock, Warminster (Wilts) (Picture, p77)

Cock & Pie, Ipswich (Suffolk)

Cuckoo, Woolaston (Northants)

Dove, Burton Bradstock (Som)

Dove & Rainbow, Sheffield (Yorks)

Eagle, Buckland St Mary (Som)

Eagle & Serpent, Kinlet (Salop)

Falcon, Fawley (Hants) (Picture, p77)

Flying Swan, Hookagate (Salop), has a most attractive sign painted from a photograph loaned by the Wildfowl Trust, Slimbridge (Glos.) (Picture, p77)

Gamecock, Cheltenham (Glos) (Picture, p77)

Gannet, near Sunderland (Durham)

Hare & Pheasant, Leicester (Leics)

Harnser, Catfield (Norfolk). The word means 'heron' in Norfolk dialect

Hen & Chicken, Bedminster, Bristol, with an attractive sign showing a hen carrying a chick on its back

Jenny Wren, Cambridge (Cambs)

Kingfisher, Chippenham (Wilts)

Nightingale, Hitchin (Herts)

Magpie & Punch Bowl, Bishopsgate, London

Moorcock, a local name for grouse. Above Garsdale (Yorks), one of the loneliest and windiest spots in England, the inn stands 1,027ft above sea level

Oadby Owl, Oadby (Leics)

Owl in the Wood, Burnley (Lancs)

Parrot, Shalford (Surrey)

Pied Wagtail, Abbey Estates, Thamesmead

Sitting Goose, Bartle, Preston (Lancs)

Sparrow, Letcombe Regis (Berks)

Swan & Bushes, Leicester (Leics)

Tern, Yate (Glos) (Picture, p77)

Three Blackbirds, Bexley (Kent)

Wild Duck, Ewen, near Slimbridge (Glos), where the Wild Fowl Trust is situated, and near Peterborough (Northants)

Woodcock, Hindhead (Surrey)

There is a *Bird's Nest*, Twickenham (Middx), and a *Bird in Hand*, North Curry (Som), with an attractive sign of a falcon (Picture, p77).

The flesh of the peacock was considered incorruptible through the ages and in Regency times a popular oath was 'by the peacock'. There are many *Peacock* inns in different parts of the country, but rare is the *Old Peacock*, Nottingham (Notts).

At the *Milford*, Yeovil (Som) there is a sign showing a Chinese, or swan goose.

In the Buttermarket, adjacent to the cathedral at Canterbury is the *Olive Branch*, which has as its sign a Noah's ark with a dove perched on it.

Fish, reptiles and insects have lent their names to inns in no small measure. There is a *Shrimp*, Morecambe (Lancs); a *Flying Fish*, Denton (Sussex); a *Three Frogs*, Woking (Berks) and even a *Shrimp & Turtle*, Sandwich (Kent). There are many a *Beehive* but more unusual is the *Beeswing*, Kettering (Northants).

TRADITIONAL AND LOCAL ASSOCIATIONS

The English inn sign has done much to keep alive local stories and traditions, as the following examples show:

Greycoat Boy, Greenwich, London, is a reminder of the famous school founded in London in 1698. The sign shows a boy with a girl on each side of Queen Anne's coat of arms, recalling that the school was once co-educational. Since 1873, however, it has been restricted to girls.

There are many *Wool Pack* inns, particularly in those areas where there was once a thriving wool trade. In the thirteenth and fourteenth centuries almost the whole economy of the country rested on the wool trade and, in the Cotswold area alone, there are a score of signs associated with the trade. Kent and Sussex were also great sheepwalks. There is a *Wool Pack* at St George, near Weston-super-Mare (Som). (Picture, p21.)

At Castleton (Derbyshire) there is a *Morris Dancers*, and at Long Preston (Yorks) a *Maypole*.

The *Stocks*, Beanham (Berks), pictures the old implement of punishment on its sign, and the ultimate penalty is shown on the macabre sign of the *Caxton Gibbet*, at Cambridge (Cambs).

The *Black Horse*, Clapton-in-Gordano (Som), was once the local 'lock-up'.

The sign of the *Lincoln Imp*, Lincoln (Lincs), reproduces the grotesque carving of the imp in Lincoln Cathedral. The mischievous demon, with long ears and only one leg, is seen in the angel choir.

The *Warren* inn, near Romney (Kent), is built on reclaimed warren land, as was Romney racecourse, famous in the eighteenth century. Each year a gold cup was presented by the Corporation, and the sign of the inn is a winning post.

The *Holy Well* stands near the hamlet of Holy Well Lake (Som), in the centre of lake villages where, hundreds of years before Christ, huts were built on platforms of timber and clay and protected by stockades.

The *Boat House*, Richmond (Surrey), is appropriately near the River Thames.

The *Old Airport*, Pengam, Cardiff (Glam), has as its sign a biplane flying over the airport.

The *Winkle* is not named after the mollusc but because of the inn's situation on the Winkleberry estate, Basingstoke (Hants).

A picture of old St Paul's is the sign of the *Ye Olde London*, which is close by the cathedral.

A three-quarter portrait of a man in mayoral robes is the sign of *Proud Salopian*, Shrewsbury (Salop). The portrait is of Colonel Southam, one time managing-director of Southam's Ales.

The *Crystal Palace*, Bath (Som), was once two private houses and at one of them Lord Nelson stayed while recovering from his wounds after the Battle of the Nile. The inn is named to commemorate the Great Exhibition of 1851. The signboard carries portraits of Albert, Prince Consort, and Nelson, with the exhibition in the background.

Another *Crystal Palace* featuring the exhibition building on its sign is at York (Yorks).

The sign of the *Whiffler*, Norwich (Norfolk), shows the man who, in a fine uniform, led medieval ceremonies and processions as does a macebearer today.

The *New Shovels*, Blackpool (Lancs), was built on the site of the old Shovels hotel. They were so-called after the clay mining operations which took place at nearby Marton Moss sometime in the last century.

Nowhere is the anniversary of Guy Fawkes's attempt to blow up Parliament in 1605 celebrated with greater jubilation and high spirits than at Bridgwater (Som). Giant squibs are specially manufactured for this annual carnival, and when a new inn was opened there its obvious name was the *Bridgwater Squib*.

Wicor Mill, Porchester, Southampton (Hants), has a windmill on its sign. (Picture, p39.)

Top (*l to r*): *Church House Inn*, Stoke Gabriel (Devon); *Star*, Bedminster, Bristol; *Lamb & Lion*, Bath (Som)
Centre (*l to r*): *Bell*, Bedminster, Bristol; *St John's*, Torpoint (Devon); *Mitre*, Crediton (Devon)
Bottom (*l to r*): *Adam & Eve*, Paradise (Glos); *Bell & Crown*, Chard (Som); *Twelve Bells*, Whitcombe (Glos)

Broad Oak, at the hamlet of that name in Sussex, has a sign showing a team of horses hauling a huge felled oak. In the same county, at the hamlet of Crossbush, near Arundel, is the *Plough & Sail*. One side of its sign features a plough with a sailing ship in the background, while the other shows a plough and the sails of a windmill.

The *Hooden Horse*, Wickhambreaux (Kent), has a quaint sign emanating from Morris dancing. (Picture, p27.)

At Hastings (Sussex), on the seafront, is the *Cutter*. In the last century the excisemen's lookout was situated on its roof, as evidenced by a print dated 1824.

The *Squirrel's Head*, Gidea Park (Essex), stands on the road to Squirrels Heath.

On the Fosseway, Newcastle upon Tyne (Northumberland), near where the first turbine engines were built, is the appropriately named *Turbinia*. The sign shows a picture of the boat which made circles round the fleet *circa* 1912.

An inn on a new estate at Wroughton, near Swindon (Wilts), commemorates the Swindon Great Western Railway works. It is the *Iron Horse* and the sign portrays a confrontation between one of the 'iron horses' and a full-blooded horse of the coaching days—symbolic of the end of one era of travel and the rise of another.

The sign of the *Terminus*, Cardiff (Glam), shows a tramcar in the glory of the Cardiff Corporation colours—a nostalgic subject for an inn which really was a terminus in the days when trams ran in the city. (Picture, p67.)

The *Bisley House*, Stroud (Glos), recalls that the nearby village of Bisley was at one time the centre of the manor and hundred of which Stroud is now a flourishing town. Sir Richard Whittington, Lord Mayor of London, was once lord of the manor, and the sign represents his shield and that of the Moarimer family who presented the common to the people of the parish for all time.

SPORTING

All forms of sport are catered for on signs, horse-racing probably being the most popular. This is particularly so in the north country, whereas in the south, fox-hunting names and signs are apt to predominate. Many signs too, refer to cockfighting and another cruel sport, bullbaiting, is the subject of signs at the *Bear*, Woodstock (Oxon), and the *Bull Ring*, Ludlow (Salop).

Examples of other sports on signs are:

Wrestlers, Cambridge (Cambs)
Kentish Cricketers, Canterbury (Kent)
Ball & Wicket, near Farnham (Surrey)
Bat & Ball, Leigh (Kent)
Coach & Eight, Newcastle upon Tyne (Northumberland), with a sign showing a rowing eight
Noble Art, London, NW3
Bowling Green, Leominster (Herefs) (Picture, p83)
The Jockey, Baughton (Worcs) (Picture, p83)
The Scales, Lichfield (Staffs), with a sign showing a jockey weighing-in
Whip & Saddle, Duns (Berwickshire)
Stag Hunters, Brendon (Som), in the yard of which the famous Exmoor pony sales are held
Stag Hunt, Ponsanooth (Cornwall)
Stag & Huntsman, Hambledon (Hants)
Jolly Fenman, Blackfen (Kent), with an angler for its sign
A particularly good *Hare & Hounds* sign is to be seen at Marple Bridge (Derbyshire)

The greatest number of signs featuring cricket are to be found in Surrey, followed by Yorkshire. Golf is represented by the *19th Hole*, Buxton (Derbyshire), others have names associated with football, hurling, hurdling, beagling and fishing.

Representing an old sport is the *Mall*, London, W8, the sign of which shows a form of croquet played in the seventeenth century.

One of the most attractive signs in the sporting category is without doubt that of the *Three Willows*, Birchanger (Essex). In silhouette style, it portrays three batsmen using 'willows', one representing eighteenth-century style, W. G. Grace the 1900 style, whilst 1946 depicts a modern style.

Rayment & Co Ltd, the brewers of Buntingford (Herts), have several cut-out signs on their houses, which include the *Coach & Horses*, Wicken Bonhunt (Essex), and the *Waggon & Horses*, Birchanger (Essex).

The *Bluebird*, Plymouth (Devon), has a sign showing the giant car in which Sir Malcolm Campbell captured the world land-speed record in 1935. He was the first motorist to exceed 300 miles per hour, which he did by just one mile per hour on the salt flats at Utah (USA). (Picture, p83.)

Another motor-age inn is the *Bugatti*, Gretton (Northants), formerly the *New* inn, with a sign featuring one of this famous Italian designer's models. The inn is the venue of the annual meeting of the Bugatti Owners' Club, when speed climbs are made on nearby Prestcott Hill. (Picture, p83.)

The *Bull*, Stratford-upon-Avon (Warks), has long been a sportsmen's rendezvous, so the name was changed to the *Sportsman* and a new sign commissioned shows a man arrayed in equipment for a number of different games. (Picture, p83.)

SPORT
ON
INN SIGNS

Sportsman, Stratford-on-Avon
(Warws)

Young Vanish, Clapwell
(Derbys)

Bowling Green, Leominster
(Herefs)

Jockey, Baughton
(Worcs)

Left: *Bugatti,*
Gretton (Glos)

Right: *Bluebird,*
Plymouth (Devon)

HUMOROUS AND PUNNING SIGNS

The *Quiet Woman* is to be found in a number of places, including Halstock (Dorset) where the sign shows the woman carrying her head.

A new slant on an old name, the *Bull & Horns*, near Gravesend (Kent), has a sign depicting a bull in a china shop.

Howlett Hall, East Denton, Newcastle upon Tyne (Northumberland), has on its sign a delightful young owl.

Monkseaton Arms, Whitley Bay (Northumberland), also has a punning sign, with a monk seated on a cannon and cannon balls.

The *Wych Way*, Brockhurst, near Gosport (Hants), has three witches on broomsticks as its attractive sign.

A Toby jug, full to overflowing, is the sign at the *Full Quart*, Hewish (Som).

The *Oystermouth*, Swansea (Glam), shows just that on its board—a caricature of an oyster with a big mouth.

One of the best punning signs is at *The Cats*, Woodham Walter (Essex). It shows several of the local 'moggies' performing their ablutions, these goodlickers underlining the fact that good liquors are obtainable at the inn.

A pig, comfortably ensconced with arms folded and looking over the side of his sty, is the appropriate sign for the *Old House at Home*, Edenbridge (Kent).

Another attractive sign is that of the *Tumbling Sailors*, Kidderminster (Worcs).

There are a number of inns with names like *Listen-inn*, *Same Yet*, *Nog inn*, *Dewdrop*, Bedford (Beds), and *Poppe Inn*, Tatworth (Som).

The sign of the *Double Barrel*, Stopsley, Luton (Beds), has the best of both worlds, for it shows two brewers' barrels *and* a double-barrelled shotgun.

At Leamington Spa (Warks), is the *Simple Simon*, which bore a more mundane name until a pie factory was opened nearby.

Maiden Over, near Newbury (Berks), has a sign showing a girl jumping over cricket stumps.

Dog in a Doublet, Crowland (Lincs), and the *Clown*, Hastings (Sussex) can both claim to be in the humorous category of inn names and signs.

At Gloucester (Glos) there is a *Mucky Duck*.

The *Bull & Butcher's* sign has a literal interpretation of its name, with a bull busy tossing the butcher.

The *Fox with his teeth drawn*, near Munden (Herts), was originally the *Fox*, but when the licence was reduced from seven days a week to six, the name was altered to the present title.

The sign of the *Copper*, Tower Bridge Road, London, SE1, shows on one side a London policeman—a 'copper'—and on the reverse a copper or boiler of the type which once came into its own in every household on wash day.

An unusual rendering of the 'Bird in Hand', usually associated with hawking or falconry, is at Bagshot (Surrey) where, at the *Bird in Hand*, the sign shows a young man with his arm round a girl.

There are many *First & Last* inns usually meaning the first hostelry in and the last out of a town. A new slant is the *Last* inn, Barmouth (Merioneth), which has as its sign a shoe on a cobbler's last.

Another humorous interpretation of an inn's name is that of the *Wild Boar* inn, Congleton (Staffs), with a sign showing a jovial boar sucking a straw and sporting a panama hat, as he leans with his forelegs over the door of his sty.

NURSERY RHYMES AND MUSICAL INSTRUMENTS

There are a number of signs under these headings, some examples being:

The *Mother Hubbard*, Loughton (Essex), the *Puss in Boots*, Hazlewood (Derbyshire), and, at Ashton (Cheshire), the *March Hare*.

Robin Hood and his merry men are to be found in various forms in different parts of the country. At Brentwood (Essex) is *Robin Hood and Little John*.

The sign of the *Jack & Jill*, Brimington (Derbyshire), shows the couple suffering their legendary mishap, and Stockport (Cheshire) has the *Tom Thumb*, with a sign featuring Tom.

Unusual is the *Hoop & Toy*, Thurloe Place, London, SW7, with a rocking horse and a child's hoop on the sign.

Among inns with musical instruments on their signs, there are the *Bugle* at Yarmouth (IOW), the *Buglehorn*, Hartwell (Bucks), the *Organ*, Worcester Park (Surrey), the *Horn & Trumpet*, Worcester (Worcs), the *Crown & Pipes*, Fen Stanton (Hunts), and the *Harp*, Abergele (Denbighshire). (Picture, p85.)

THE WORLD OF LITERATURE

Inns have always featured prominently in literature and have often been a source of inspiration to authors. Charles Dickens used dozens in his tales and many of his characters are now commemor-

An unusual sign at Abergele (Denbighshire)

in 1465, was in use until the seventeenth century. Worth 6s 8d in its earliest days, and later valued at 14s 1d, it carried the figure of the Archangel Michael.

Another unusual interpretation is that of the *White Bear*, Bedale (Yorks), where the sign portrays a galleon seen through a torn sail. The ship, built in 1564, was one of Sir Francis Drake's squadron which 'singed the king of Spain's beard' in 1587. A plaque inside the inn records the historical details.

Near the old Princes theatre, Manchester, was an inn named *Princes*. When the sign faded the landlord, one Tommy Ducksworth, employed an itinerant painter to re-embellish it and add his name. The artist started with gusto but his lettering was far too large, with the result that he could only accommodate Tommy Ducks, so the *Tommy Ducks* it has been ever since.

The *Bulldog*, Oxford (Oxon), has a sign showing not the breed of dog, but the university official who carries that nickname.

Passers-by may well look surprised when they pass the *One and Three* inn, Oldham (Lancs). There is, however, a simple explanation—it is number 13 in the street.

The name of the *Mitre*, Tonbridge (Kent), is said to be a corruption of 'martyr'. The district had predominantly Royalist sympathies in the Civil War, and there is the church of King Charles the Martyr close by.

In the West Country there are many inns called *Berkeley* after the family of that name, and it might well be assumed that one in the North Country had similar associations. In fact, a 'berkeley' is a clearing in a wood and the brewers, having canvassed local suggestions, called their inn at Burton-on-Trent (Staffs) the *Berkeley*.

The *Bank of England*, Ancoats, Manchester (Lancs), was so-named as a compliment to the landlord whose honesty and straight dealing were such that he was deemed as 'safe as the Bank of England'.

Some inn names seem to defy logical explanation but are often the result of an amalgamation of two inns. The *Lamb & Packet*, Preston, (Lancs), is a typical example of two names being joined in the hope of enjoying double custom. The *Beetle & Wedge*, Moulsford (Berks), on the other hand,

ated in names of inns or on their signs. One such is the *David Copperfield*, Rochester (Kent).

Poets have had inns named after them and the *Cross Keys*, in the Scottish border town of Peebles, was frequented by Sir Walter Scott, who used it as the prototype of the Cleikum inn of his 'St Rowan's Well', published in 1823. Marian Ritchie, mine hostess at that period, became Meg Dods of the tale.

At Wimborne (Dorset) there is the *Sir John Barleycorn*.

Jack o'Lantern, South Ockendon (Essex), takes its name from the Jack o'Lantern, or Will o' the Wisp, a flamelike phosphorescence flitting over marshy ground.

An attractive pictorial sign decorates the *Merrie Wives of Windsor*, Windsor (Berks), while the *Peldon Rose*, near Colchester (Essex), figures in Baring Gould's novel 'Mehala'. Originally built in the sixteenth century, the inn was badly damaged by an earthquake in 1884.

NOT WHAT THEY SEEM

Inn names do not always have the meaning one might expect, and a typical example is the *Angel*, Birch (Essex), where the sign shows a gold coin. It represents the angel-noble which, first minted refers to tools, the beetle being a heavy wooden mallet used for splitting logs.

Other odd names derive from those of local districts which, though familiar to residents, must often puzzle visiting strangers. As, for instance, the *Deerplay*, Bacup (Lancs), and the *Moses Gate* and the *Doffcocker*, two inns in districts of Bolton (Lancs).

Right in the centre of the industrial heart of Bristol and surrounded by factories and busy roads is the *Pride of the Forest*.

A corruption of the carpentry term 'rebates' is said to have been the reason for the *Rabbits*, Stapleford Tawney (Essex), and the 'budget' in the name of the *Tinker & Budget*, Oswaldtwistle (Lancs), was a little sack, containing food and stock-in-trade, which itinerant tinkers carried over their shoulder on the end of a stick.

The sign of the *Old Crown*, Hayes (Middx), depicts the now vanished five-shilling piece of that name anciently stamped with a crown. An ancient oak tree once stood on the site of the present inn when the area was covered by the forest of Kingswood.

The *Dog & Bacon*, Horsham (Sussex), is a corruption of 'Dorking Beacon', which can be seen on a clear day from Horsham, and for more years than the 'locals' can recall the *Red Lion*, Burnley (Lancs), was known as the *Big Window*, now the official name of the inn.

The crocodile which adorns the board of the inn of that name at Danehill (Sussex) is no reptile but a set of tongs, known as 'crocodiles', such as were used by smugglers in the eighteenth century. The *Crocodile* inn is 600 years old, and at one time the surrounding marshland was a popular haunt of smugglers who found it a useful area in which to hide their contraband. When it was safe to retrieve it, they used the long tongs which were kept at the inn to hook the goods out of the mud. These crocodiles are now valuable antiques and command a high price on the rare occasions they come on to the market.

The flower, not the cigarette, is the subject of

The largest inn in the British Isles, the *Swan* at Yardley, Birmingham, with a drinking area of 13,852 square feet

—And the smallest, the *Smith's Arms*, Godmanstone (Dorset), with an area
of only 200 square feet

the attractive sign at the *Woodbine*, Epping Forest
(Essex), and nearby is the *Old Hainault Oak*, situated in Hainault Forest on ancient woodland which
was disafforested in 1851 At Hainault also is the
Old Maypole.

LARGEST AND SMALLEST INNS

From a drinking area of some 200sq ft to one of
13,852sq ft is no mean jump, but that would appear
to be the difference between the smallest and the
largest inns of Great Britain.

At Godmanstone (Dorset) the *Smith's Arms* is
believed to be the smallest, measuring only 20ft by
10ft, with the eaves just 4ft from the ground. The
Downham Tavern, near Bromley (Kent), opened
in 1930, was until a year or so ago the largest, but
has now apparently been superseded by the mother
and father of all inns, the *Swan*, Yardley, Birmingham. Built in 1967, these are the vital statistics:

The *Swan* has eight bars, plus an á-la-carte restaurant
and steak bar
Its total drinking area is 13,852sq ft
Permanent staff total approximately sixty, of whom
seven live in a flat over the pub

The pub can accommodate well over 1,000 customers
in all
Beer sold is equivalent to 31,000 bottles a week
The banqueting room and ballroom can accommodate
400 people for buffet and dancing, and up to 320
for banquets
The pub has at least 1½ miles of beer piping and
the cellars hold nearly 25,000 pints on tap.

It is an Allied Breweries Ansells establishment.

Until fairly recently the inn with the longest
name was the *13th Mounted Cheshire Rifleman*,
Stalybridge (Ches) with twenty-seven letters. The
word 'mounted' has now been deleted, leaving only
twenty letters. The title must seem now to go to *Ye
Olde Tippling Philosopher* with twenty-five letters.

SOME NEW NAMES AND
MODERN BUILDINGS

Brewers and innkeepers have usually been reluctant to rename inns or alter signs, but in recent
years one brewery, at least, has made a clean
sweep of its *New* inns, most of which are usually
quite old or built on the site of previous ones, and
some welcome originality is now being shown in
the choice of names.

Two years after the assassination of John Kennedy, 35th President of the United States, the Aylesbury Brewery Co organised a competition to find a suitable name for a new inn they were about to open at Meadowcroft, Aylesbury (Bucks). *John Kennedy* was the final selection, and the sign, surely the only one in this country, carries a portrait of the late president.

Opened in 1956, the *Top of the World*, near Warner's End, Hemel Hempstead (Herts), commemorates the Everest expedition of 1953. The sign is based on the well-known photograph of Sherpa Tensing standing on the summit.

The *Dovecot*, Billericay (Essex), is unique in being shaped like a traditional dovecot. The bars inter-connect on different levels and are appropriately named, one being known as the 'Seed Box'.

Near the Tottenham Hotspurs' ground in North London is an inn well abreast of the times with a sign showing a large 'P' and the head of a parking-meter.

The landlord's hobby resulted in the renaming of the *Grapes*, Dover (Kent). An enthusiastic jazz player, leading his own band at the inn, he decided to call his house the *Louis Armstrong*, and a portrait of the famous American musician, complete with trumpet, appears as the sign.

The first completely circular hotel in Europe was the *Ariel*, erected close to London Airport early in the 1960s. It takes its name from the first steam-powered aircraft, 'Ariel', which was invented and patented in 1842 by a Somerset engineer. The lounge bar has a sedate Victorian atmosphere.

Lone Yachtsman, Plymouth (Devon), honours both Sir Francis Chichester and Sir Alec Rose. There is a 'Gipsy Moth' bar downstairs and a 'Lively Lady' upstairs, thus commemorating both yachts.

A year or so ago, when a name was needed for a new inn at Blackburn (Lancs), Blackburn Rovers football team had been relegated to the second division and the hopes of all its supporters were pinned on an early return to the first division. So it was that the *Rover's Return*, not without considerable opposition from local residents, became the name of the new inn. Oddly enough, the name of the builder was the same as that of Len Fairclough, the character in the television programme 'Coronation Street', and so Peter Adamson, who plays the name

part in the series, performed the opening ceremony.

The City of Bristol has many mementoes of the great engineer, Isambard Kingdom Brunel (1806–59). These include Temple Meads station, the suspension bridge and, more recently the ss *Great Britain* has come to rest in the city. In 1972, a new inn, the *Brunel*, was opened by the great man's great-great-grandson, Sir Marc Noble.

The *Cruel Sea*, a Finch's house in London, NW3, was so named after Nicholas Monserrat's best-selling novel about the Royal Navy in World War II. The inn was officially opened by the author and the decor of the bars is in a nautical style.

The *Clanger* at Houndsditch, London, has as its theme the Great Fire of London of 1666, the clanger being the motif after the fire bells.

Another inn whose name has recently been changed is the *Crown*, Tolpuddle (Dorset), the village where, in 1834, six agricultural labourers tried to form a trade union. Their action was condemned as a conspiracy in restraint of trade and they were transported to Australia, but pardoned two years later. In 1971, the village inn was renamed the *Martyrs*, the ceremony being performed by the General Secretary of the Trades Union Congress.

The *Tower*, Redhill (Surrey), has a sign showing the London Post Office tower, the connection being that Redhill is the principal GPO centre for that area of Surrey.

Though recently rebuilt and thoroughly modernised, the old *Prince Regent*, Stepney, East London, fortunately retains its old name. The bars display framed prints of various cavalry, infantry and naval uniforms of the Regency period.

In 1968, Watney Mann & Co opened an inn with a completely new approach. It was the *Bird's Nest*, at Twickenham (Middx). Designed to cater especially for the 18–25 age group, the main characteristics are dance floor, disc jockeys and individual tables with telephones which can be used for requesting records, ordering food or communicating with other tables. The two-sided sign shows a bird on a nest with four eggs and, on the reverse, a kingfisher with a fish in its beak.

Samuel Pepys (1633–1703) is perhaps best known

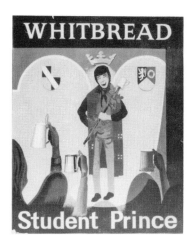

Top (*l to r*): *Pear Tree*, Charfield (Glos); *Mousetrap*, Bourton-on-the-Water (Glos); *Balance*, Luston (Herefs)
Centre (*l to r*): *Cat & Custard Pot*, Shipton Moyne (Wilts); *Weighbridge*, Longford (Glos)
Bottom (*l to r*): *Student Prince*, Luton (Beds); *Four Seasons*, Yate (Glos); *Quiet Woman*, Halstock (Dorset)

for his diaries, for he lived through and recorded such momentous events as the Restoration, the Plague, the Fire of London and the Dutch Fleet sailing up the Thames. He was also first secretary of the Admiralty and president of the Royal Society.

The *Samuel Pepys* was opened by Charrington's at Brooks Wharf, near Upper Thames Street, in 1968, after part of a warehouse had been splendidly converted into a smart riverside pub. The decor reflects three aspects of Pepys: Admiralty official, diarist and romantic. The downstairs chandlers' bar, with its paved floor, has been designed to create the atmosphere of a working warehouse, and shows the signs and wares of various merchants who supplied the navy in Pepys's day.

His romantic life is recalled in the restaurant, where the tables are set in curtained alcoves named after the inns and taverns where he discreetly took his lady loves. Five are set in a facsimile four-poster bed, recalling his oft-quoted saying, 'And so to bed'. In the restaurant an extensive á-la-carte menu includes some of Pepys's favourite dishes, such as pigeon pie and apple fritters, and the waitresses wear period costumes. The outside sign is a small one, but a bust of Samuel, himself, stands above the entrance.

There is also a *Samuel Pepys* at Gillingham (Kent).

AND STILL THEY COME

There seems no end to the variety of names that enterprising brewers and owners give to their inns. Some of the many which defy classification include:

Haunch of Venison, Wilton (Wilts), a fourteenth-century inn
Shoulder of Mutton, Oswaldtwistle (Lancs)
Round of Beef, Colley Gate (Worcs)
Hood & Horse, Littlebourne (Kent)
Ancient Shepherd, Bolton (Lancs)
Baltic Fleet, Burnley (Lancs)
Norway, Perranarworthal (Cornwall). A Viking ship is on the sign

Rising Moon, Matley (Cheshire)
Half Moon, Warninglid (Sussex)
Sun & Star, Westhill (Surrey)
Friend at Hand, Aylesbury (Bucks), has a delightful sign of a shepherd holding a small lamb in his arms
Happy Man, Stapleford (Notts)
Perseverance, Woolwich, London
Rest & Welcome, Melbury Osmond (Dorset)
Jester, near Leeds (Yorks)
Mermaid. New and attractive signs at Paignton (Devon) and Christian Malford (Wilts) (Picture, p27)
Cotton Tree, Bolton (Lancs)
Cobweb, Boscastle (Cornwall)
Gipsy's Tent, Bolton (Lancs)
Talisman, Hitchen (Herts)
Butt & Oyster, Pin Mill (Suffolk)
Chimney Corner, Kempston Hardwick (Beds)
Hat and Feathers, Cambridge, (Cambs)

And some, even more unusual:

Coffee Pot, Yardly Gabon (Bucks)
Black Venus, Challacombe (N Devon)
Pin Cushion, Wyberton, Holland (Lincs)
Angel's Reply, Hitchen (Herts)
Shrew Beshrewed, Hersden, near Canterbury (Kent)

And perhaps the most charming:

Flowering Spring, Shiplake (Oxon)
Pot of Flowers, Stowmarket (Suffolk)
Four Seasons, Yate (Glos), where the sign depicts the four seasons in humorous form (Picture, p89)
Dark Lantern, Aylesbury (Bucks), with the sign showing a lantern standing on a barrel
Tumble Beacon, Banstead (Surrey)

Finally, where better than the *Fusilier*, formerly the *Cemetery*, Darwen (Lancs), for that 'last round' before the landlord's ominous call of 'Time gentlemen, please!'

PART III

And Associated with Inns

THE STORY OF THE COGERS

The history of the Cogers—the oldest debating society in London and possibly in the whole country—is closely connected with the story of many inns and taverns within the city of London.

The society was founded by Daniel Mason, a freeman of the Tallowchandlers Company, at the old *White Bear* tavern, Bride Street, in the City of London in 1755. A minute of the year 1793 records:

> The Society originally consisted of Citizens of London, who meet to watch the course of political events, and the conduct of their representatives in Parliament.
> The objects of the Society are: The promotion of the Liberty of the Subject, and Freedom of the Press. The maintenance of Loyalty, to the Laws, the rights and claims of Humanity, and the practice of Public and Private Virtue. Debates are open to *all*, members, or not.

The last survivor of the eighteenth-century coffee house and tavern debating societies, the Cogers' continuing existence, despite many changes of meeting place, is a tribute to the hold its particular form and atmosphere have had upon successive generations of members. This is even more remarkable since, unlike so many other city institutions, it owns no property, has had no rich bequests, and has always resisted the creation of any formal financial structure, relying instead on the generosity of its members to overcome problems as they arise.

Coming into existence at a time when the reporting of Parliamentary affairs was a penal offence and the gathering of news a difficult and lengthy process, it provided a forum in which a vigorous exchange of views on all kinds of subjects could take place, and this it does to this day.

The proceedings of the society are unique. There is no formal written constitution or set of rules, no resolution or motions are taken or debated, and as no one may speak twice from the rostrum, though interruption from the floor is permitted, there is no right of reply. A member, or visitor, may stroll in or out at any time, eat or drink, interrupt or listen, subject only to the general tolerance of the meeting. Such a society was bound to attract in its time many independent spirits, not a few of whom have left their mark on English life.

The only time a Cogerian evening has ever been curtailed was when the society had moved to Upper Thames Street and was debating the recent removal of Oliver Cromwell's statue from Westminster Hall and the suggestion that it should never be replaced. One elderly Coger made such an impassioned defence of Cromwell that the audience cheered him as he left the rostrum. It was his last contribution for, on taking his seat, he died.

Many distinguished men of letters have been members in the two hundred years of the society's existence, including Dr Johnson, Oliver Goldsmith, Macaulay, Bradlaugh, and T. P. O'Connor. Charles Dickens was a member and it is recorded in an old journal that many of his characters were drawn on men he met at the meetings. There was a Dick Swiveller to the life, and a frothy writer named Piper, was the original Simon Tappertit.

The name of the society is derived from the Latin *cogito* and the motto is '*Cogito, ergo sum*' (I think, therefore I am).

The society left the *White Bear* in 1856, and its next meeting-place was in Shoe Lane, then on to the *Barley Mow* in Salisbury Square. Through its long history other taverns which from time to time have served as headquarters are the *Cock* tavern, Fleet Street, the *Dyer's Arms*, Cannon Street, the *Peacock*, Maiden Lane, the *White Lion*, Lower Thames Street, and the *White Horse*, Fetter Lane.

The society, which meets every Saturday evening to debate the events occurring in a changing world, carried on through the two world wars, in the last of which it was twice bombed out. On one occasion at the *Red Lion*, off Fleet Street, blast from a bomb blew out all the windows and brought the ceiling down. The speaker was interrupted but by no means cast down. Dusting himself down, he calmly completed his speech.

The noisy, almost informal meetings still go on, with people carrying on conversations, heckling and getting their drinks during the proceedings. There is no admission charge or annual subscription.

Truly a genuine piece of old England with all the conviviality and friendliness which has hall-marked the English inn from its inception. And so long as there are inns may there continue to be Cogers to keep alive their ancient tradition.

THE BRITISH PUB INVADES THE CONTINENT AND THE NEW WORLD

For hundreds of years British pubs have had no counterpart elsewhere in the world, but British brewers in recent years have been looking further afield and the first pub on English lines was opened in Paris in 1965 by Watney Mann and appropriately named the *Sir Winston Churchill*.

Whitbreads, too, have been enthusiastic in their efforts to establish the English pub in Paris and in the last few years have opened no less than nineteen in that city. All of them have the name of their British parent over the door, though each bears a special name. English beer accounts for the bulk of sales, fittings, decor and design are mainly British, and only the customers are predominantly French.

Opening hours differ from those in England, for some are open all night and the majority do not close until the early hours.

Their names are an odd mixture of English and French, and include:

St Michel, opposite Notre Dame and on the quayside of the Left Bank. Its three floors are really cellars, for flooding of the Seine caused the embankment to be raised by two storeys

Piccadilly, the smallest pub in Paris, right in the heart of the Latin quarter

Magenta. The interior is crammed with antiques and bric-a-brac mostly picked up in London's Portobello road

La Tour D'Argent, where there has been a licensed house since 1450

Pub Store. A curious combination of pub, cafe, boutique and delicatessen

Le Dreher. Theatrical and Edwardian decor

Royal. Meeting place of the Bohemians

St Germain. Open twenty-four hours a day

Stock Exchange, the walls of which are covered with prints of bulls and bears, and the menus are imitations of British share certificates

Except for the street names these pictures could have been taken in one of a dozen places in London. In fact, the *Cockney* is a Courage pub in Paris

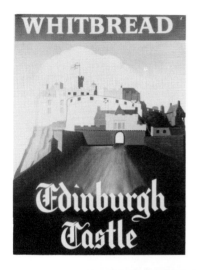

Left: *Edinburgh Castle*,
San Francisco, USA

Right: *Ye Olde Tudor Inn*,
Dusseldorf, Germany

Mayflower, Kennedy Airport,
New York, USA

Wellington, Dusseldorf,
Germany

BRITISH

INN SIGNS

ABROAD

Left: *The Whitbread Pub*,
Belfort, Germany

Right: *The Rock*,
Gibraltar

An interior view of the *Cockney*, in Paris

Others include the *Lafayette, St James, Gambetta, Rivoli Park, East Regent, Pub Club,* and *Cormoran.*

There is also a Courage house in Paris rejoicing in the name of the *Cockney.*

In Belgium, Watneys have nine English pubs, most of them with typically English names. There are five in Brussels—*Queen Victoria, Winston & Kipling, Swan, Red Lion* and *Schuman.* At Antwerp there is another *Red Lion,* and the *Oliver Twist;* at Ghent, the *York Arms,* and at Ostend, the *Clipper.*

Finch's of London opened their first pub in Amsterdam in 1972, and were fortunate in securing a building of historic character and traditional atmosphere. Its title and address is *Amstel 100.* Built about 1637, it is a typical example of seventeenth-century Dutch domestic architecture and arranged on the traditional plan of two buildings, a warehouse at the front and the owner's dwelling-house at the rear, separated by a small courtyard. Immediately behind *Amstel 100* is another courtyard which accommodates the smallest chapel in Amsterdam. Originally known as St George's Court, the influence of the Reformation caused the Catholic-inspired name to be changed to Swegthers' Court—Isaac Swegthers having been a part-owner of the house.

Whitbread's first venture into Italy was named the *Lord Nelson*—not surprisingly when his love affair with Lady Hamilton and the honours which a grateful King of Naples showered upon him are recalled. The pub, which is at Chiavari, near Rapallo, has an interior decor which recalls the admiral's quarters on HMS 'Victory'. Murals depict his great battles at Copenhagen, the Nile and Trafalgar. There is an effective display of battle

plans. The same company also has the *Duke's Head* in Milan. In Germany, there is the *Wellington,* and *Ye Olde Tudor,* both at Dusseldorf. (Picture, p93.)

The Golden Egg group's first overseas venture was a pub in Zurich, Switzerland, and another followed at Geneva. Whitbreads have the *Londoner* in Paris, Allied Breweries have their *English Pub* at Lille, France, and the *Double Diamond* at Rotterdam, Holland, while Bass Charrington have a *Pickwick* at Geneva, Switzerland, and two others in Stockholm, Sweden.

Another wholly English pub is at Honfleur, France, where actor Peter Churchill designed and restored the place now named the *Ivanhoe.* It is situated in the heart of old Honfleur, a town with English associations dating back to the time of the Vikings. The 'Enclos' (walled fortress) as it was known, was ruled by English governors, one of whom was Sir John Falstaffe, for a period of thirty years from 1429. A complete and accurate record of the events of this period are preserved in a collection of private documents known as the Toublet-Breart Collection, extracts from which are displayed in the pub.

On the famous Rock of Gibraltar, Courage have the *Horseshoe,* whilst Whitbreads have two English pubs, the *Royal Oak* and *The Rock.* (Picture, p93.)

Similar ventures have taken place in North America, where Whitbreads have the *Mayflower,* at the BOAC International terminal, Kennedy Airport, New York, with a decor in Tudor style. There is also the *Edinburgh Castle* in San Francisco, the meeting place and headquarters of many Scottish organisations, and appropriately owned by an immigrant from Scotland. (Picture, p93.)

The Sign Painters

The painters of inn signs in days gone by were men of varying talent. Some signs were executed by first-rate artists such as William Hogarth and David Cox, but these were rare. More often men listed as coach painters—who emblazoned the crests and arms on the panels of coaches—painted inn signs as a side line. There were, too, a host of itinerant artists who were as glad to paint a sign in return for a drink and a meal as the innkeeper was to have a sign on the cheap.

In the early part of this century men began to specialise in the work and many breweries set up their own departments but, possibly as the result of so many amalgamations, few brewery companies today have their own specialist staffs. The Whitbread Flowers group has possibly the largest self-contained department for sign painting but most other big companies now largely rely upon freelance artists specialising in this work.

It is impossible to list all these specialists, but

two of the top men in very different spheres may serve as examples.

John Cook, company artist of Whitbread Flowers Ltd, has been a painter of signs since he was sixteen years of age. A pupil of the late Charles Sansome of the Stroud Brewery, he considers himself fortunate to have been trained by such a great craftsman in strict traditional methods, and he also studied at the Stroud School of Art under the late Gwilym Jones. A Territorial, John Cook served throughout World War II as a Royal Artillery surveyor on forward flashspotting observation posts, seeing action in Tunisia and Italy.

The war over, he returned to Stroud where he established a pictorial sign studio for the Stroud Brewery, which later joined the Whitbread group. He later recruited a band of fellow enthusiasts, who now include Michael Hawkes, Robert Simmonds, Nicholas Robertson and Graham Watkins, who work not as individuals but as an enthusiastic team.

For forty years now, John Cook has been researching, designing and painting inn signs, and the work, he asserts, has been more than rewarding in the appreciation it has afforded him of traditional crafts, fine art, heraldry and history. A member of the Heraldry Society, with an extensive heraldic library built up over the years, he is also a Fellow of the Royal Society of Arts and a former member and first honorary friend of the Guild of Gloucestershire Craftsmen.

One may be sure that when one of his signs is hung it is as accurate as intensive research can make it, as witness the *Sedgemore* sign, which brings the battle alive, the coat of arms at the *Pelham*, and the *Cheeserollers* which, with its mixture of ancient lore and humour, is a natural 'stop-and-stare' sign.

All the signs which have come from his studio must now constitute a veritable 'Everyman's National Gallery', and are to be seen and enjoyed not only in the Midlands, Wales and the West, but as far afield as the Waldorf Astoria and Kennedy Airport, New York; San Francisco, Europe, and wherever Whitbread International extends. No wonder that within (and indeed outside) the organisation no one ever refers to John Cook, but only to 'Rembrandt'. Married, he lives in the Stroud valley in the Cotswolds and has one daughter.

Stanley Chew is a freelance sign artist. He was educated at Dulwich College and then went on to Beckenham Art School, where he recalls the fees were then £12 per year. It is characteristic of the man that he thrived at art school, for there, as he put it, he was free of the surburban snobbery which even now leaves him a little distrustful of clean collars. In his third year he won a studentship to the Royal College of Art and in his last year there he painted a sign for the *Hoop & Toy* inn, Kensington, London, but it was only an exercise and it was twenty years before he painted another.

A Territorial, like John Cook, he attended camp in August 1939—a 'camp' which was fated to last for six years and seven months, during which he served both as a sapper and a gunner. He claims to have become probably the most senior lieutenant in the Army, being considered far too outspoken for further promotion.

The war over, he was twenty-eight years of age and started to try and earn his living. He lived in a bombed-out coachhouse in Bromley (Kent), and was employed as a commercial artist by a firm of industrial advertisers whose premises were off Fleet Street. He learnt a little about accuracy but lack of daylight and a wage of £5 made it necessary to put in overtime at freelance work. Soon he took the plunge and went freelance completely, but after a few months suffered a nervous breakdown. Leaving London, he became a farm worker in the Cotswolds and then, deciding to take up farming seriously, he went to an agricultural college. Eventually he became a farm manager, but his old love was calling and he took up his art work again. Appalled by the standards of many inn signs in which, though the lettering was usually good the pictures were poor, he made trial sketches for one or two and then painted a good one which he hawked round as a sample.

With a smallholding of his own by the side of the river Dart in Devon, he now has an excellent connection but it is his boast that, no matter how flourishing the sign business is, he still milks his cows twice a day and, as he says, finds the earthy side fits in well with fiddling with paint. He has four sons—all are following crafts of some kind.

Stanley Chew is of a very independent turn of mind. He does not suffer fools gladly but, between his studio overlooking the Devon countryside and his livestock, he is happier now than he has ever been, and his many excellent signs bear witness both to his artistry and craftsmanship.

The *Giles*, Islington, London. Opened in 1973. The sign is a copy of a specially drawn cartoon by Giles, the famous 'Daily Express' cartoonist, who was born at the *Angel*, opposite the new inn. The signboard is the work of Whitbread Flowers Studio, Cheltenham (Glos)

97

A competition sponsored by John Smith's Tadcaster Brewery Company Ltd, brought in 700 entries which gave the judges quite a problem. Two of the judges above: the author and (right) Mr R. S. Rowe, Director of Leeds City Art Gallery

An attractive animal sign at Stoke-sub-Hamdon (Som)

Increasingly popular are interior murals. This excellent example measuring 4ft by 5ft, depicts a scene at the battle of Waterloo, at *Waterloo House*, Bridgwater (Som)
The painting by Stanley Chew

ACKNOWLEDGEMENTS

The author wishes to tender his sincere thanks and appreciation to all who have supplied information for this book. The collection of the material has been spread over a number of years and innumerable people have been of help in various ways.

Especially appreciated, has been the assistance and courtesy of the brewery companies in answering queries. They include : —

Adnams Brewery, Sole Bay Brewery, Suffolk

Ansells Ltd, Aston Brewery, Birmingham

Aylesbury Brewery Co Ltd, Walton Brewery, Aylesbury, Bucks

Beard & Co (Lewes) Ltd, Lewes, Sussex

Brewers Soc, London

Charrington & Company Ltd, London, E1

Courage (Eastern) Brewery, Horselydown, London, SE1

Finch, H. H. Ltd, London, E1

Golden Egg Group

Ind-Coope Ltd, Burton-on-Trent, Staffs

Rayment & Co Ltd, Butingford, Herts

Robinson, Frederic, Ltd, Stockport, Cheshire

Russell Cobb Ltd, Watneys

St George Taverns Ltd, Albion Brewery, London, E1

Smiths, John, Tadcaster Brewery, Tadcaster (Yorks)

Smith, Saml, Old Brewery (Tadcaster) Ltd, Yorks

Swallow Hotels, Sunderland, Co Durham

Theakston, T. & R. Ltd, Masham, Yorks

Threlfalls (Liverpool & Birkenhead) Ltd

Thwaites, Daniel, & Company Ltd, Star Brewery, Blackburn, Lancs

Truman Ltd, The Brewery, London, E1

Watney Mann Ltd, London, SW1

Welcome Inns Ltd, Fownhope, Hereford

Wells, Charles, Ltd, The Brewery, Bedford

Whitbread & Co Ltd, Chiswell Street, London, EC1

Whitbread Flowers Ltd, Cheltenham, Glos

My thanks also extend to John Cook, Chief Artist, Whitbread Flowers Ltd, and Stanley Chew, Artist, specialising in Inn Signs, of Buckfastleigh (Devon); Harlow Development Corporation (Essex)

General Index

Names of Inns appear under a separate Index

Absinthe, 30
Addison, Joseph (poet), 54
Adelaide, Queen, 80
Afghan War, 70
Agricultural and Countryside, 76
Ahmed, Khel, Battle of, 72
Air Travel, 69
Alamein, Battle of, 10
Albert, Prince Consort, 80
Alfred, King, 22, 23
All Saints Church, Newcastle-upon-Tyne (Northumb), 23
Alma, Battle of, 74
American astronauts, 26
American National Anthem, 24
American War of Independence, 70
Amsterdam (Holland), 95
Ancient customs, 33, 51, 80
Animals, Birds, Fish and Reptiles, 76
Anne, Queen, 17, 18, 22, 64, 80
Archer, Fred, 59
'Ark Royal' Aircraft carrier, 74
Arun, river, 61
Asquith, H. H., 20
'Atmospheric' Railway (S Devon), 9, 47
Attlee, Earl, 65

Badajoz, Siege of, 24
Bader, Group Capt Douglas, RAF, 10
Balaclava, Battle of, 74
Ballooning, 69
Barber-Surgeons Company of London, 44
Barbers' pole, 74
Battle names on signs, 10
Battles and Campaigns
  Ahmed Khel, 72
  Alamein, 10
  Alma, 74
  Balaclava, 74
  Battle of Britain, 10, 45, 48, 59
  Copenhagen, 70, 95
  Crécy, 64
  Culloden, 17, 28
  Gibraltar, 74
  Hastings, 47
  Inkerman, 74
  Malta, 74
  Nile, 17, 80, 95
  Odessa, 74
  Poitiers, 61
  Relief of Mafeking, 19
  Sebastapol, 74
  Sedan, 33
  Sedgemoor, 22, 59
  Towton, 47

  Trafalgar, 70, 95
  Waterloo, 23, 24, 70, 99

Belgian pubs, 95
Beeching, 'axe', 40
'Bellerophon', HMS, 17
Benbow, Admiral, 34
Benskin, Joseph, 29
Berkeley Castle (Glos), 35
Bexley, Baron, 34, 65
Billingsgate fish market, London, 59
Bilsdale Hunt (Yorks), 25
Bishops Rock lighthouse, 42
Black Prince, 64
Blackburn Rovers FC, 88
Blackfriars, London, 19
Blake, Admiral Robert, 70
Blenheim Palace, 22
Boer War, 70
Bonnie Prince Charlie, 28
Boxstead (Essex), 12
Brewers
  Allied Breweries, 95
  Ansells Ltd, 52, 54, 56
  Aylesbury Brewery Co Ltd, 40, 80
  Beard & Co (Lewes), 40
  Benskin's Watford Brewery Ltd, 29
  Cannon Brewery, 29
  Charrington & Co Ltd, 90, 95
  Cobbold Ltd, 52
  Courage Brewery, 95
  Finch, H.H. Ltd, 88, 95
  Golden Egg Group, 95
  Ind Coope Ltd, 29, 65
  Pantons Wareham Brewery, 29
  Portsmouth & Brighton United Breweries, 20
  Rayment & Co Ltd, 82
  Robinson, Frederic, Ltd, 64, 70
  Smith's, John, Tadcaster Brewery, 98
  Stroud Brewery, 56, 96
  Thwaites, Daniel & Co, 50
  Vaux Breweries, 14
  Watford Brewery Ltd, 29
  Watney Mann Ltd, 88, 92, 95
  Wells, Charles, Ltd, 55
  Whitbread & Co Ltd, London, 51, 57, 61, 72, 92, 95
  Whitbread East Pennines, 61
  Whitbread Flowers Ltd, 57, 95, 96, 97
  Whitbread International, 96
  Whitbread Wales, 58
Bristolware, 19
Britain, Battle of, 10, 45, 48, 59
'British Inn Signs and Their Stories', 10
British Museum, 38, 54
Brontë sisters, 33

Broughton Castle (Oxon), 57
Brunel, Isambard Kingdom, 47, 88
Bull baiting, 82
Bullnose Morris Club, 18
Bunyan, John, 65
Burns, John, 20
Campbell, Sir Malcolm, 82
Canterbury Cathedral, 64
Carmelite Monastery, 33
Casabianca, Admiral, 17
Categories of signs, 62-90
Catherine the Great, Empress of Russia, 44
Chandos, Baron, 65
Chard canal, 35
Charles I, 17, 18, 34, 37, 62, 74
Charles II, 42, 44, 56, 59, 62, 64, 65
Chartists, 12, 65
'Chesapeake' episode, 50
Chew, Stanley (inn sign artist), 23, 26, 44, 66, 96, 99
Chichester, Sir Francis, 88
Chichester-Selsey tramway (Sussex), 17
Chislehurst (Kent), 33
Chorley Wood (Herts), 9
Civil War, 19, 34, 54, 57, 62, 64, 70, 85
Coaching era, 17, 32
Coal mines under the sea, 9
Cobden, Richard, 51
Cockermouth (Cumb), 9
Cockfighting, 51
Cockpit, Stamford (Lincs), 17
Coel, King, 16
Cogers Society, 91
Colchester (Essex), 16
Colchester Museum (Essex), 16
Collier, John (poet), 52
Columbus, Christopher, 9, 32
Competition for inn signs, (illus), 98
'Concorde', 10, 43
Continent, new pubs, 92
Cook, John (sign artist), 51, 72, 96
Copenhagen, Battle of, 70, 95
Cornwallis, Marquis of, 70
Cotswolds, 10, 56, 80
Cotswold wool trade, 80
Coverdale, Miles, 22
Cox, David (artist), 42, 95
Crécy, Battle of, 64
Crimean War, 74
Crystal Palace, 66
Culloden, Battle of, 17, 28
Cumberland, Duke of, 17, 44
Cunningham, General, 10
Cunobelin, Iron Age king, 16

'Dairymaid' coach, 38
Danotty Hall, nr Thirsk (Yorks), 14
Dart, river, 55
Dartmoor granite, 54
Defoe, Daniel, 79
De Hoghton family, 25
Delhi, Siege of, 70
Denmark, King of, 17
Department of Environment, 9, 50
Devonshire Great Consolidated Mining Co, 46
Dickens, Charles, 18, 33, 35, 84, 91

Dimsdale, Thomas, 44
Dissolution of the monasteries, 11, 23, 33
Dominican Religious Order, 19
Drake, Sir Francis, 18, 85
Dutch pubs, 95

Edward the Confessor, 62
Edward II, 35
Edward III, 28, 62, 64
Edward VI, 24
Edward VII, 32, 57
Elizabeth I, 26, 42, 62
Everest expedition, 88
Exe, river, 9, 47

Falconry, 84
Family coats of arms, 64
Festival of Britain 1951, 25
Fielding, Henry (novelist), 23
Fire of London, 59, 88, 90
Fleming, Ian Lancaster, 58
Fletcher, John, 65
Fortescue, Sir John, 47
Franklin, John, 70
French Revolution, 19
Fruiterers Company, 62

Gaiety Theatre, London, 22
'Gallows' (or Beam) signs, 10
Gaumont Cinema, Finchley, London, 24
George I, 23, 65
George III, 30, 58
George IV, 64
George V, 64
German pubs, 95
Ghosts, 11, 14, 52, 56, 61
Gibraltar, Battle of, 74
Gibraltar, pubs on, 95
Gibson, Wg Cmdr Guy, vc, 10
Gilbert, Sir William S., 22
Giles, C. R. (cartoonist), 97
Glasson Dock, 50
Gloucester Cathedral, 32
Godiva, Lady, 66
Gomm, Sir William M., 28
Gordon Riots, 48
Grace, W. G., 82
Granby, Marquis of, 70
Great Fire of London, 59, 88, 90
'Great Harry' flagship, 30
Grenville, Sir John, 42
Grenville, Sir Richard, 26
Grey, Lady Jane, 32
Grimaldi, Joseph, 46
'Growler', 10
'Gurkha' HMS, 32
Gurkha regiment, 32
Guy Fawkes, 80

Hackney Canal, 54
Hadrian's Wall, 69
Hallowell, Capt Benjamin, 17
'Hansom Cab', 10
Harlow New Town (Essex), 36
Hastings, Battle of, 47

Hawkhurst smuggling gang, 38
Haworth (Yorks), 12
Haymarket Theatre, London, 9
Henry II, 54
Henry III, 41
Henry IV, 28
Henry VIII, 23, 30, 38, 62, 64, 65
Hereditary Earls Marshal, 64
Hereward the Wake, 23
Herring, John F. (animal painter), 61
Herringsgate Farm, Rickmansworth (Herts), 12
Highwayman, the last, 38
History from inns, 9
Hitler, Adolf, 74
Hogarth, William, 23, 95
Honfleur, France, 95
House of Commons Select Committee, 12
'Hovercraft', 10
Humorous and Punning Signs, 84

'Impulsoria' invention, 9, 38
Indian Mutiny, 32, 70
Inkerman, Battle of, 74
Inns as landmarks, 9
International Veteran & Vintage Car Rally, 18
'Introduction to Inn Signs', 10
Ipswich Museum (Suffolk), 52
Italian pubs, 95

Jacobite Rebellion, 41
James I, 23, 65
James II, 59
Jeffreys, Judge, 19, 59
Jolliffe family, Merstham (Surrey), 17

Kennedy, John, 88
Kent River Authority, 16
Killigrew, Sir Robert, 23
Kings and Queens
    Adelaide, 80
    Alfred, 22, 23
    Anne, 17, 18, 22, 64, 80
    Charles I, 17, 18, 34, 37, 62, 74
    Charles II, 42, 44, 56, 59, 62, 64, 65
    Denmark, King of, 17
    Edward the Confessor, 62
    Edward II, 35
    Edward III, 28, 62, 64
    Edward VI, 24
    Edward VII, 32, 57
    Elizabeth I, 26, 42, 62
    George I, 23, 65
    George III, 30, 58
    George IV, 64
    George V, 64
    Grey, Lady Jane, 32
    Henry II, 54
    Henry III, 41
    Henry IV, 28
    Henry VIII, 23, 30, 38, 62, 64, 65
    James I, 23, 65
    James II, 59
    Napoleon Bonaparte
    Napoleon III, 33
    Richard I, 62
    Richard II, 64, 65

    Victoria, 64, 66
    William the Conqueror, 23, 47, 60
    William III, 17
    William IV, 28, 64
King's School, Bruton (Som), 26
Knaresborough (Yorks), 26
Knights Templar, 41
Kossuth, Louis, 65

Labrador dog, 57, 79
Lake villages (Som), 80
Lambert, Daniel, 17
Lambeth Walk dance, 48
Land Drainage Act, 16
Largest and Smallest Inns, 87
Lawrence, Sir Thomas, 20
Layer-de-la-Haye (Essex), 11
League of Nations, 30
Lincoln Cathedral, 80
Lind, Jenny, 30
Literature, World of, 84
London Livery Companies
    Barber – Surgeons, 44
    Basketmakers, 10
    Clockmakers, 10
    Furniture makers, 10
    Gold and Silver Wyre Drawers, 10
    Horners, 10
    Innholders, 10
    Joiners and Ceilers, 10
    Loriners, 10
    Pewterers, 10
    Scriveners, 10
    Tallow-chandlers, 10
    Tanmakers, 10
    Upholders, 10
    Upholsterers, 10
Longest name, 87
Lonsdale family, 9
Lord, Thomas, 65
Lords Bailiff & Jurats of Romney Marsh (Kent), 16
Lord's Cricket Ground, 65
'L'Orient', French flagship, 17
Luddite Riots, 28
Lyndhurst, Baron, 28

Mafeking, Relief of, 19
Malta, Battle of, 74
Marlborough, Duke of, 22, 50
Martello Towers, 28
Massacre of Glencoe, Argyle (Scotland), 28
Mazzini, Giuseppe, 65
Monmouth, Duke of, 59
Monument, London, 26, 59
Morris Oxford and Cowley cars, 18
Mother Shipton predictions, 26
Music Hall, beginning of, 24
Musical instruments, 84
'My Fair Lady', 65

Napoleon Bonaparte, 70, 74
Napoleon III, 33
Napoleonic Wars, 24, 65
National Land Co, 12
Naval and Military, 70
Nell Gwynne, 56, 65

GENERAL INDEX

Nelson, Lord, 17, 19, 58, 59, 70, 80
New Names and Modern Buildings, 87
New York (USA) pub, 95
Nidd, river, 26
Nile, Battle of, 17, 80, 95
North American pubs, 95
'North Star', engine, 69
North-West Frontier, 72
Number of inns in British Isles, 10
Nursery rhymes, 16, 30, 84

O'Connor, Fergus (chartist), 12
Odessa, Battle of, 74
Oldest inns, 17, 54
Orange, Prince of, 64
Order of the Garter, 22
Ouse, river, 18
Oxford, City of, 18

Palmerston, Lord, 65
Paris (France) pubs, 92, 95
Paxton, Sir Joseph, 66
Penn, William, 23
Pennsylvania, USA, 24
Pepys, Samuel, 59, 88
Picton, Sir Thomas, 24
Pilgrim traffic, 62
Piltdown skull, 50
Plains of Abraham (Canada), 70
Plaques, 60
Poitiers, Battle of, 61
Politicians, 64
Poor Law Commissioners, 14
Portsmouth, Earls of, 48
Post Office Tower, London, 88
Prince Imperial of France, 33
Prince Regent, 64
'Pygmalion', 65

Railway era, 68
Railways
   Bristol & Exeter, 35
   Chatham & Dover, 69
   Great Eastern, 69
   Great Western, 52
   Liverpool & Manchester, 68
   London, Brighton & South Coast, 18
   London & South Western, 38
   London, Tilbury & Southend, 69
   South Eastern, 69
   South Western, 48
   Stockton to Darlington, 68
   West London, 47
Raleigh, Sir Walter, 23
Rawdon, General, 10
Reformation, 22
Regimental Signs, 72
Religious Signs, 62
Restoration, 24, 44, 70, 90
Richard I, 62
Richard II, 64, 65
Rickmansworth (Herts), 12
Rivers
   Arun, 61
   Dart, 55
   Exe, 9, 47

Nidd, 26
Ouse, 18
Tamar, 44
Teign, 54, 55
Thames, 29, 59, 90
Wye, 23
Roberts, Lord, 70
'Rocket', 69
Roman settlement, Colchester (Essex), 16
Roman Stone, London, 59
Romney Marsh (Kent), 16
Rose, Sir Alec, 88
RAF Fighter Command, 48, 59
Royal Arms, 62
'Royal George' HMS, 30
Royal and Heraldic Signs, 62
Royal Mail coaches, 54, 66
Royal Naval College, Dartmouth (Devon), 70
Russell, Revd Jack, 48
Rye (Sussex), 38

St Crispin, 40
St George's Church, Stamford (Lincs), 22
St John's Church, Blackburn (Lancs), 62
St Mary's, Isles of Scilly, 42
St Paul's Cathedral, 20, 50
St Thomas's Hospital, London, 44
San Francisco (USA) pub, 95
Saye & Sele, Lord, 57
Schorne, John, 40
Schrivenham Church (Berks), 20
Science Museum, London, 66
Scott, Sir Walter, 17, 85
Sebastapol, Battle of, 74
Sedan, Battle of, 33
Sedgemoor, Battle of, 22, 59
Services provided by inns, 9
Shaw, Bernard, 65
'Sheffield' HMS, 58
Ships, 69
Sign painters, 95
Simon de Montfort, 38
Smallest inn, 87
Smuggling, 51, 54
Smuggling in Sussex, 61
Society of Friends (Quakers), 23, 50
Soho, London, 29
South Shields (Co Durham), 14
Space travel, 26, 69
Spanish Armada, 58
Spithead, 30
Sporting, 82
Star of India (Victorian Order), 16
Starcross (Devon), 9, 47
Stokes, Lord, 65
Stories of Inns, 11–61
Stover Canal, 54
Street numbering, 9
Sullivan, Sir Arthur, 22
Swedish pubs, 95
Swiss pubs, 95

Tamar, river, 44
Tavistock Canal, 46
Tavistock mines (Devon), 44
Teign, river, 54, 55

Thames, river, 29, 59, 90
Titanic disaster, 37
Tolpuddle martyrs, 88
Topsham (Devon), 9
Tower of London, 59
Towton, Battle of, 47
Trades and Callings, 74
Trafalgar, Battle of, 70, 95
Trans-Antarctic Expedition, 44
Transport featured on signs, 10
Travel and Transport, 66
Tyler, Wat, 65

USA, British pubs in, 95
Utick (or Yutick), 11

Van Dyck, 37
Vauxhall Gardens, London, 59
Vernon, Admiral, 10
Victoria, Queen, 64, 66
Victoria and Albert Museum, London, 34
'Victory' HMS, 17, 58, 95

Walpole, Sir Robert, 65
Wars
    Afghan, 70
    American War of Independence, 70
    Boer War, 70
    Civil, 19, 34, 54, 57, 62, 64, 70, 85
    Crimean, 74
    Napoleonic, 24, 65
    North-West Frontier, 72
    Spanish Armada, 58
    Wars of the Roses, 47
    World War I, 72
    World War II, 22, 48, 58, 74, 88, 96
    Zulu, 33

Warwick, Countess of, 57
Waterloo, Battle of, 23, 24, 70, 99
Waterlooville (Hants), 23
Welcome Inns Ltd, 23
Wellington, Duke of, 23, 70
Wellington Memorial (Som), 70
Westbury, Lord, 65
Westminster Abbey, 41, 70
Westonbirt Arboretum (Glos), 65
Wey-Arun Canal, 61
Whately, William (Puritan divine), 47
Whitehaven (Cumb), 9
Wilberforce, William, 41
Wild Fowl Trust, Slimbridge (Glos), 79, 80
William the Conqueror, 23, 47, 60
William III, 17
William IV, 28, 64
Wilson, Richard (RA), 42
Wolfe, James, 70
Wolf Rock lighthouse, 42
Wolsey, Cardinal, 65
Woolwich Dockyard, 30
Woolwich Military Academy, 33
World War I, 72
World War II, 22, 48, 58, 74, 88, 96
Wren, Sir Christopher, 59
Wyatt Rebellion, 65
Wye, river, 23

York, Duke of, 64
Yutick (or Utick), 11

Zulu War, 33

Index of Inns

Almost all the names in the following list are followed by **Arms, Tavern** or something similar. For convenience and quick reference, unless there is a special reason only the title is mentioned here. Bold figures indicate illustrations.

Adam & Eve, Newbury (Berks), 62
Adam & Eve, Paradise (Glos), 62, **81**
Admiral Benbow, Milton (Berks), 35
Admiral Benbow, Shrewsbury (Salop), 34
Admiral Cunningham, Fareham (Hants), **63**
Air Balloon, Brockworth (Glos), 69
Alma, 74
Amstel 100, Amsterdam (Holland), 95
Anchor, 62
Ancient Briton, Colchester (Essex), 16
Ancient Shepherd, Bolton (Lancs), 90
Angel, Birch (Essex), 85
Angel, Islington, London, 97
Angel, Wetherby (Yorks), 62
Angel & Crown, Highbury, London, 62
Angel's Reply, Hitchen (Herts), 90
Anglesea Arms, Orpington (Kent), 64
Anvil, Warley (Worcs), 76
Apple Tree, Cockermouth (Cumb), 9
Ariel, nr London Airport, 88
Ark Royal, Plymouth (Devon), 74
Artichoke, Christow (Devon), 9
Ash, Tiy Green (Essex), 32
Ashburton Arms, West Charlton (Devon), **53**, 64
Atmospheric, Starcross (Devon), 47
Auctioneers, Weasham (Leics), 74
Avon Inn, Avonwick (Devon), **53**
Avondale, Devonport (Devon), **39**

Badger & Fox, Annesley (Notts), 79
Bailiffs' Sergeant, St Mary's Bay (Kent), 16
Baker & Oven, Twickenham (Middx), 76
Baker's Arms, Chipping Campden (Glos), **73**
Balaclava, Blackburn (Lancs), 74
Balance, Luston (Herefs), **89**
Balancing Eel, South Shields (Co Durham), 14
Ball & Wicket, nr Farnham (Surrey), 82
Baltic Fleet, Burnley (Lancs), 90
Bank of England, Ancoats (Lancs), 85
Barge Aground, Barking (Essex), 22
Barrington Arms, Shrivenham (Berks), 20
Bat & Ball, Leigh (Kent), 82

Bear, Bisley (Glos), **55**, 56
Bear, Devizes (Wilts), 20, 79
Bear, Woodstock (Oxon), 22, 82
Beehive, 80
Beehive, Yeovil (Som), **78**
Beeswing, Kettering (Northants), 80
Beetle & Wedge, Moulsford (Berks), 85
Bell & Dragon, Cookham (Berks), 55
Bell, Bedminster, Bristol, **81**
Bell & Crown, Chard (Som), **81**
Berkeley, 85
Berkeley, Burton-on-Trent (Staffs), 85
Bettel & Chisel, Delabole (Cornwall), 76
Bicycle, Rotherfield (Sussex), 69
Big Window, Burnley (Lancs), 86
Bird in Hand, Bagshot (Surrey), 84
Bird in Hand, North Currey (Som), 77, 80
Bird's Nest, Twickenham (Middx), 80, 88
Bishop & Wolf, Isles of Scilly, **41**, 42
Bisley House, Stroud (Glos), 82
Black Bush, Cockermouth (Cumb), 9
Black Dog, Newent (Glos), 57, **57**
Black Dog, Weymouth (Dorset), 79
Black Friar, London, 19
Black Horse, Bristol, **78**
Black Horse, Clapton in Gordana (Som), 80
Black Horse, Pluckley (Kent), 61
Black Lion, Plaistow (Essex), 79
Black Prince, Farnham (Surrey), 64
Black Rabbit, Arundel (Sussex), 61
Black Robin, Kingston-on-Thames (Surrey), 79
Black Swan, Langport (Som), 79
Black Venus, Challacombe (Devon), 90
Blackboys, Uckfield (Sussex), 50
Blacksmiths Arms, Plymtree (Devon), **73**
Bladud Arms, 28
Bladud's Head, 28
Blake Arms, Bridgwater (Som), 70
Blind Beggar, Whitechapel Road, London, 38
Blossoms, Chester (Ches), 76
Blue Bird, Plymouth (Devon), 82 **83**
Blue Bowl, Polsham (Som), 19, **39**
Boat House, Richmond (Surrey), 80
Bombay Grab, London, E3, 35
Boot Inn (Hunts), 40
Boot Inns (Beds), 40

Boot Inns (Bucks), 40
Bowling Green, Leominster (Herfs), **83**
Bowlturners, Leicester (Leics), 76
Brick & Tile, Eigh, Ash Green (Essex), 74
Brickmakers, Barons Cross (Herfs), **73**, 76
Brickmakers' Arms, Blackburn (Lancs), 11
Bridge, Yatton (Som), 38, **67**
Bridgwater Squib, Bridgwater (Som), 80
Britannia, Hackney, London, 69
Britannia, Truro (Cornwall), **21**
British Flag, Bridgwater (Som), **71**
British Flag, Gloucester (Glos), 70
Broad Oak, Broad Oak (Sussex), 82
Brown Bear, Devonport (Devon), 79
Brown Cow, Cockermouth (Cumb), 9
Brunel, Bristol, 88
Brushmakers, Upham (Hants), 74
Buckinghamshire Yeoman, Aylesbury (Bucks), 72
Buckle, Seaford (Sussex), 28
Bugatti, Gretton (Northants), 82, **83**
Bugle, Yarmouth (IOW), 84
Bugle Horn, Hartwell (Bucks), 84
Bulkeley Arms, Anglesea, 64
Bull, **75**, 79
Bull & Butcher's, 84
Bull & Horns, nr Gravesend (Kent), 84
Bull & Mouth, St. Martins le Grand, London, 66
Bull & Tiger, Boreham Wood (Herts), 79
Bulldog, Oxford (Oxon), 79, 85
Bulldog, Waltham Cross (Herts), 79
Bullfinch, Innsworth (Glos), 79
Bullnose Morris, Oxford (Oxon), 10, 18, **18**
Bull Ring, Ludlow (Salop), 82
Bull's Head, Guildford (Surrey), 57
Bun Shop, Cambridge (Cambs), 36
Bunch of Carrots, Hampton Bishop (Herfs), 23
Burmese Cat, Melton Mowbray (Leics), 79
Busby Stoup, Thirsk (Yorks), 9, 14
Bush, Cockermouth (Cumb), 9
Butt & Oyster, Pin Mill (Suffolk), 90
Butter Churn, Carshalton (Surrey), 76
Byron House, Bath (Som), 65
Cannon, Ash (Hants), 72
Cannon, London, 59

Canopus, Rochester (Kent), 69
Cape Horner, Swansea (Glam), 69
Captain Cook Inn, Staithes (Yorks), **49**
Cardinal, Woking (Surrey), 65
Caribou, Glasson Dock, Lancaster (Lancs), 50
Carpenters, Dundry (Som), **73**, 74
Carters Rest, Wroughton (Wilts), 68
Case is Altered, 50
Castell y Bwch, Henllys (Mon), **31**
Castle Eden, Durham (Co Durham), **31**
Cat & Custard Pot, Shipton Moyne (Wilts), 79, **89**
Cats, The, Woodham Walter (Essex), 84
Cat's Whisker, Childwall (Lancs), 79
Cavendish, **53**
Caxton Gibbet, Cambridge (Cambs), 80
Cemetery, Darwen (Lancs), 90
Centurion, Bicester (Oxon), 48
Centurion, Lincoln (Lincs), **71**
Chainmakers, Cradley Heath (Worcs), 74
Chainmakers, Walsall (Staffs), 74
Chairmakers, Worlds End (Hants), 78
Chalk Drawers, Olney Heath (Bucks), 74
Chandos, London, W, 65
Chatham & Dover Railway, London, SW11, 69
Cheese Rollers, Shurdington (Glos), **45**, 51, 96
Chequers, Lytchett Matravers (Dorset), 35
Chimney Corner, Kempstone Hardwick (Beds), 90
Church House, Stoke Gabriel (Devon), 62, **81**
Churchill, West Lavington (Wilts), **63**
City of Ramsgate, Wapping, London, 59
Clanger, Houndsditch, London, 88
Clem Attlee, Fulham, London, 65
Cleveland Bay, Redcar (Yorks), 79
Clipper, Ostend (Belgium), 95
Clown, Hastings (Sussex), 84
Coach & Eight, Newcastle-upon-Tyne (Northumb), 82
Coach & Horses, 66
Coach & Horses, Chislehampton (Oxon), 66
Coach & Horses, Clifton, Bristol, **67**
Coach & Horses, Portsmouth (Hants), 20
Coach & Horses, Wicken Bonhunt (Essex), 82
Coal Exchange, Fareham (Hants), 61
Cobweb, Boscastle (Cornwall), 90
Cock, London, 59
Cock, Warminster (Wilts), **77**, 79
Cock & Pie, Ipswich (Suffolk), 79
Cockney, Paris (France), **92**, **94**, 95

Coeur de Lion, Bath (Som), 62
Coffee Pot, Yardley Gabon (Bucks), 90
Colliers, Radcliffe, nr Manchester (Lancs), 74
Comet, 10
Coopers, Ashton, Bristol, 74
Copper, London, SE1, 84
Cormoran, Paris (France), 95
Cormorant, Portchester (Hants), 44
Cornubia, Redruth (Cornwall), 64
Cotton Tree, Bolton (Lancs), 90
Coverdale, Paignton (Devon), 22
Cow & Calf, Romiley (Cheshire), 76
Crab Tree, Adlyfield (Herts), 76
Cranford, Exmouth (Devon), **77**
Crimea, Castleford (Yorks), 74
Crispin, Woolaston (Northants), 40
Crocodile, Danehill (Sussex), 86
Cross Keys, Peebles (Peebles), 85
Crown, Arnside (Westmor), 51
Crown, Capel (Surrey), 62
Crown, Ibberton (Dorset), **21**
Crown, Minchinhampton (Glos), 66
Crown & Pipes, Fen Stanton (Hunts), 84
Crown & Treaty, Uxbridge (Middx), 34
Cruel Sea, London, NW3, 88
Crystal Palace, Bath (Som), **27**, 80
Crystal Palace, York (Yorks), 80
Cuba, 74
Cuckoo, Woolaston (Northants), 79
Cupid, Hemel Hempstead (Herts), 19
Curfew, Bath (Som), 19
Cutter, 82
Cutter, Hastings (Sussex), 82
Cyprus, 74

Dairy Maid, Aylesbury (Bucks), 9, 40, 66
Dark Lantern, Aylesbury (Bucks), 90
Dartmoor, Lydford (Devon), 18
David Copperfield, Rochester (Kent), 85
Deerplay, Bacup (Lancs), 86
Desert Rat, Reigate (Surrey), 74
Devil's Stone, Shebbear (Devon), **45**
Dewdrop, Bedford (Beds), 84
Dimsdale Arms, Hertford (Herts), 44
Distressed Sailors, Whitehaven (Cumb), 9
Doffcocker, Bolton (Lancs), 86
Dog & Bacon, Horsham (Sussex), 86
Dog & Badger, Clophill (Beds), 79
Dog & Badger, Medmenham (Bucks), 79
Dog & Partridge, nr Stockport (Ches), 76
Dog in a Doublet, Crowland (Lincs), 79, 84
Dog Tray, Brighton (Sussex), 43
Dolphin, Ilminster (Som), 76, **78**
Donkey & Buskins, Layer-de-la-Haye (Essex), 9, 11

Dook, Falmouth (Cornwall), 70
Double Barrel, Luton (Beds), 84
Double Diamond, Rotterdam (Holland), 95
Dove, Burton Bradstock (Som), 79
Dove & Rainbow, Sheffield (Yorks), 79
Dovecot, Billericay (Essex), 88
Downham Tavern, Bromley (Kent), 87
Drill, Gidea Park, London, 74
Drinker Moth, Harlow New Town (Essex), 36
Drum & Monkey, Stamford (Lincs), 56
Drunken Duck, Hawkshead (Lancs), 43
Duke of Bedford, Hawkesbury Upton (Glos), **63**
Duke of Cornwall, Stoke-sub-Hamdon (Som), 64
Duke of Monmouth, Bridgwater (Som), **63**
Duke of Wellington, 70
Duke of York, Horfield (Glos), 64
Duke's Head, Milan (Italy), 95
Duke without a Head, Wateringbury (Kent), 9, 42
Duncombe Arms, Hertford (Herts), 65

Eagle, Buckland St Mary (Som), 79
Eagle, Ross-on-Wye (Herefs), 26, **27**
Eagle & Serpent, Kinlet (Salop), 79
East Regent, Paris (France), 95
Eastgate, Cowbridge (Glam), **39**
Ebrington Arms, Ebrington (Glos), 47, **53**
Eclipse, Tunbridge Wells (Kent), 66
Edinburgh Castle, San Francisco, USA, **93**, 95
Edward VII, Rushden (Northants), 64
Edward VII, South Littleton (Worcs), 64
Elephant & Castle, 50
Elephant's Head, Hackney, London, 79
Eliza Doolittle, Euston Road, London, 65
Elm Tree, Radstock (Som), **31**
Engine, Newcastle-upon-Tyne (Northumb), 69
Engine & Tender, St Neots (Hunts), 69
Engineers, Henlow (Beds), 74
English Pub, Lille (France), 95
Escape, London, **37**, 37
Essex Skipper, Harlow New Town (Essex), 36
Ethelbert, Herne Bay (Kent), 62

Falcon, Fawley (Hants), **77**, 79
Falkland Arms, Great Tew (Oxon), 64

INDEX OF INNS

Fallow Buck, Enfield (Middx), 79
Farmers Arms, St Brides Major (Glam), **75**, 76
Farriers, 66
Ferrie, Symonds Yat (Herefs), **39**
Fighting Cocks, nr Burnley (Lancs), 34
Fire Engine, Bristol, 69
First & Last, 84
Five Horseshoes, 66
Fleece, Birtsmorton (Worcs), **13**
Fleece (Glos), 10
Fletchers Arms, Angmering-on-Sea (Sussex), 65
Fleur de Lys, Yeovil (Som), **21**
Flowering Spring, Shiplake (Oxon), 90
Flower Pot, Remenham (Berks), 76
Flowers of the Forest, London, 76
Flying Bull, Rake (Hants), 66
Flying Fish, Denton (Sussex), 80
Flying Lancaster, Desford (Leics), 69
Flying Machine, Biggin Hill (Kent), **58**, 59
Flying Monk, Malmesbury (Wilts), 69
Flying Saucer, Gillingham (Kent), 69
Flying Scud, Haggeston, London, 20
Flying Scud, Plaistow, London, 22
Flying Shuttle, Farnworth (Lancs), 76
Flying Swan, Hookagate (Salop), **77**, 79
Forces, Dittisham (Devon), 74
Fountains, Canterbury (Kent), 24
Four Alls, 26
Four Horseshoes, 66
Four Seasons, Yate (Glos), **89**, 90
Fox & Hounds, Eggesford (Devon), 48
Fox & Hounds, Hungerford Bottom (Hants), 43
Fox & Hounds, St Brides Major (Glam), **78**
Fox with his teeth drawn, Munden (Herts), 84
Friend at Hand, Aylesbury (Bucks), 90
Frigate, St Martins Lane, London, 69
Full Moon, Bedminster, Bristol, **77**
Full Moon, Bristol, 76, **78**
Full Quart, Hewish (Som), 84
Furnham, Chard (Som), 35, **39**
Fusilier, Darwen (Lancs), 90

Gambetta, Paris (France), 95
Gamecock, Cheltenham (Glos), 77, 79
Gamekeeper, Compton Dando (Som), 74, **75**
Gannet, nr Sunderland (Durham), 79
Gardeners, nr Blackburn (Lancs), 74
Garden Tiger, Harlow New Town (Essex), **36**, 36
Garland Ox, Bodmin (Cornwall), 79 **63**
Garrick's Head, Cheltenham (Glos),
Gate, Upper Braills (Warks), **13**
Gaydons, Barnstaple (Devon), **45**
General Gordon, Nelson (Lancs), 70

General Wolfe, Westerham (Kent), 70
George, 62
George, Abbotsleigh (Som), **21**
George, Bathampton (Som), **27**
George, Stamford (Lincs), 17
George, Wedmore (Som), 23
George & Blue Boar, Holborn, London, 66
Gibraltar Castle, 74
Gilbert & Sullivan, London, 22
Giles, The, Islington, London, **97**
Gipsy's Tent, Bolton (Lancs), 90
Glassmakers, Bromsgrove (Worcs), 74
Globe, Cockermouth (Cumb), 9
Gloucester Flying Machine, Gloucester (Glos), 66
Glue Pot, Swindon (Wilts), 52
Golden Arrow, Folkestone (Kent), 69
Golden Cross, Twyford (Berks), 62
Golden Hind, Musbury (Devon), **49**
Golden Swift, Harlow New Town (Essex), 36
Goldfinger, Highworth (Wilts), **31**, 59
Good Samaritan, Ramsbottom (Lancs), 62
Gordon Arms, Fareham (Hants), **71**, 74
Grapes, 76
Gravediggers, Portsmouth (Hants), 16
Grave Maurice, London, 64
Great Harry, Hemel Hempstead (Herts), 30
Great Harry, St. Albans (Herts), 30
Great Northern, 68
Great Western, 68
Great Western, Yeovil (Som), **67**
Great Western, Warwick (Warks), 69
Green Dragon, Combe St Nicholas (Som), 76, **78**
Green Dragon, Hardraw (Yorks), 76
Green Dragon, Kirkby Lonsdale (Westm), 76
Green Lion, Rochester (Kent), 79
Greycoat Boy, Greenwich, London, 80
Grey Mare, Oswaldtwistle (Lancs), 76
Gun, Deptford, London, 59
Gurkha, Iver (Bucks), 32

Half Butt, Great Horkesley (Essex), 76
Half Moon, Milford (Surrey), 70
Half Moon, Stamford (Lincs), 22
Half Moon, Stoke-sub-Hamdon (Som), **98**
Half Moon, Warninglid (Essex), 90
Hammer & Pincers, Wymeswold (Leics), 76
Hand & Shuttle, Padiham (Lancs), 74, 76
Happy Landings, Knowle, Bristol, 69
Happy Man, Stapleford (Notts), 90
Hare & Hounds, Marple Bridge (Derbys), 82
Hare & Pheasant, Leicester (Leics), 79
Harnser, Catfield (Norfolk), 79

Harp, Abergele (Wales), 84, **85**
Harrier, Hamble (Hants), 69
Harvesters, Galhampton (Som), 75, 76
Hat & Feathers, Cambridge (Cambs), 90
Hatters, nr Stockport (Ches), 74
Haunch of Venison, Wilton (Wilts), 90
Haw Bridge, Tirley (Glos), **39**
Hawk & Buckle, Llannefydd (Denbigh), 14
Haycock, Wandsford (Northants), 57
Heart & Club, Harlow New Town (Essex), 36
Hearts of Oak, Barnstaple (Devon), **71**
Hearts of Oak, Drybrook (Glos), **31**, 57
Hen & Chicken, Bristol, 79
Henry Fielding, Dunball, nr Bridgwater (Som), 23
Hero, 70
Hero of Waterloo, 70
Hero of Waterloo, Portsmouth (Hants), 23
Highwayman, Skelmersdale New Town (Lancs), 38
Hobbs Boat, Lympsham (Som), 60
Hole in the Wall, Colchester (Essex), 16
Holford Arms, Knockdown, Tetbury (Glos), **53**, 65
Holy Well, Holywell Lake (Som), 80
Honeypot, Queensbury, North London, 76
Hood & Horse, Littlebourne (Kent), 90
Hooden Horse, Wickhambreaux (Kent), **27**, 82
Hoop & Toy, London, SW7, 84, 96
Hop Pole, Cheltenham (Glos), 43, **75**
Hope & Anchor, Hope Cove (Devon), 62
Horn & Trumpet, Worcester (Worcs), 84
Horse & Cart, Peasmarsh (Sussex), 66
Horse & Groom, 66
Horse Guards, Tillington (Sussex), 74
Horseshoe, Gibraltar, 95
Hour Glass, Exeter (Devon), 23
Hour Glass, Nelson (Lancs), 23
Howard Arms, Ilmington (Glos), **53**, 64
Howlett Hall, East Denton (Northumb), 84
Hoy, Greenwich, London, 69
Humming Bird, Harlow New Town (Essex), 36
Hurlers, Haworth (Yorks), 12

Ilchester Arms, nr Shepton Mallet (Som), 64
Imperial Arms, Chislehurst (Kent), 33
Imperial Forces, Chatham (Kent), 74
Indian Queens, Indian Queens (Cornwall), 66

Inkerman, 74
Iron Duke, 70
Iron Horse, Wroughton (Wilts), **67**, 82
Ivanhoe, Honfleur (France), 95
Ivor Arms, Portllanfraith (Mon), **53**

Jack & Jill, Brimington (Derbys), 84
Jack-in-the-Green, Rockbeare (Devon), **27**
Jackal, Thurleigh (Beds), 79
Jack o' Lantern, South Ockendon (Essex), 85
Jack Russell, Swinbridge (Devon), 48
Jacobs Ladder, Stratton (Wilts), 62
Jenny Lind, Hastings (Sussex), 30
Jenny Lind, Sutton (Surrey), 30
Jenny Wren, Cambridge (Cambs), 79
Jester, nr Leeds (Yorks), 90
Jockey, Baughton (Worcs), 82, **83**
John Bunyan, Little Common (Herts), 65
John Kennedy, nr Aylesbury (Bucks), 88
Jolliffe Arms, Merstham (Surrey), 17
Jolly Brewer, 76
Jolly Cockney, Lambeth, London, **46**, 48
Jolly Collier, Radstock (Som), 74
Jolly Coopers, Flitton (Beds), 74
Jolly Fenman, Blackfen (Kent), 82
Jolly Thresher, Lymm (Cheshire), 76
Jolly Weavers, Banbury (Oxon), 74
Joseph Benskin, Watford (Herts), 28

Kentish Cricketers, Canterbury (Kent), 82
Keystone, Rickmansworth (Herts), 24
Kicking Cuddy, Bowleese (Co Durham), 79
Kicking Donkey, Burwash (Sussex), 79
Kicking Donkey, Dunmow (Essex), 79
Killigrew Arms, Falmouth (Cornwall), 23
King Alfred, Burrowbridge (Som), **15**, 23
King Charles, Bristol, 64
King Coel, Colchester (Essex), 16
Kingfisher, Chippenham (Wilts), 79
King Edward VII, Longlevens (Glos), **15**, 64
King George V, High Wycombe (Bucks), 64
King William, Shepton Mallet (Som), **15**, 64
Kings Arms, Cheltenham (Glos), **21**
Kings Arms, Crewkerne (Som), **21**, 64
Kings Arms, Montacute (Som), 64
King's Arms, Stow-on-the-Wold (Glos), 64
Kings Head, Bledington (Glos), **15**
Kings Head, Chigwell (Essex), 35
King's Head, Colchester (Essex), 16
King's Head, Hursley (Hants), **15**

King's Head, Wateringbury (Kent), 62
Kings Head, Wells (Som), 15
King's House, Glencoe (Argyll), 28
Knife & Cleaver, Houghton Conquest (Beds), 76

La Tour D'Argent, Paris (France), 92
Lad in the Lane, Erdington, Birmingham (Warks), 54
Lady Godiva, Coventry (Warks), 66
Lafayette, Paris (France), 95
Lamb (Glos), 10
Lamb, Great Rissington (Glos), **78**
Lamb & Flag, 62
Lamb & Lion, Bath (Som), **81**
Lamb & Packet, Preston (Lancs), 85
Lambeth Walk, London, 48
Land o' Cakes, Manchester (Lancs), 56
Land of Liberty, Chorley Wood (Herts), 9, 12
Last, Barmouth (Merioneth), 84
Laughing Fish, Isfield (Sussex), 40
La Dreher, Paris (France), 92
Leather Bottell, Lewknor (Oxon), 76
Leathern Bottel, Cranfield (Beds), 76
Leathern Bottel, Wavendon (Bucks), 76
Leopard's Head, Blackburn (Lancs), 79
Lettered Board, Pickering (Yorks), 30
Lincoln & Imp, Lincoln (Lincs), 80
Listen-Inn, 84
Little Pig, Bromsgrove (Worcs), 79
Lobster Smack, Canvey Island (Essex), 76
Locomotive, 68
Locomotive, Ashford (Kent), 76
Locomotive, Newton Abbot (Devon), **67**
Loggerheads, Gwernymynydd (Flint), 42
Londoner, Paris (France), 95
London Stone, London, 59
Lone Yachtsman, Plymouth (Devon), 88
Lord Bexley, Bexleyheath (Kent), 33, 65
Lord Crewe Arms, Blanchland (Northumb), 11
Lord Hill, Uxbridge (Middx), 70
Lord Lyndhurst, Peckham Rye, London, 65
Lord Nelson, Chiavari (Italy), 95
Lord Nelson, Dartmouth (Devon), 70
Lord Nelson, Ilminster (Som), **63**
Lord Nelson, Norton-sub-Hamdon (Som), 70
Lord Palmerston, Highgate, London, 65
Lord Roberts, Sandy (Beds), 72
Lord Stokes, Leyland (Lancs), 65
Lord Westbury, Wandsworth Road, London, 10, 65
Louis Armstrong, Dover (Kent), 88

Mafeking Hero, Bishops Waltham (Hants), 19
Magenta, Paris (France), 92
Magpie, Stonham (Suffolk), 10
Magpie & Punchbowl, Bishopsgate, London, 79
Magpie & Stump, Old Bailey, London, 48
Maiden Over, nr Newbury (Berks), 84
Mail Cart, Spalding (Lincs), 68
Mall, London, W8, 82
Malta, 74
Malt Scoop, 76
Man in Space, Stoke on Trent (Staffs), 70
Man on the Moon, Birmingham (Warks), 70
Man on Wheels, Luton (Beds), 33
Manor House, West Bromwich (Staffs), 56
March Hare, Ashton (Cheshire), 84
Margaret Catchpole, Ipswich (Suffolk), 52
Marlow, Marlow (Bucks), 69
Marquis, Rhosybol (Anglesea), 70
Marquis of Cornwallis, Bethnal Green, London, 70
Marquis of Cornwallis, Finsbury, London, 46
Martyrs, Tolpuddle (Dorset), 88
Mayflower, New York (USA), **93**, 95
Maypole, Long Preston (Yorks), 80
Merchants, Blackburn (Lancs), 74
Merchants, Bristol, 74
Mermaid, Christian Malford (Wilts), 90
Mermaid, Paignton (Devon), **27**, 90
Mermaid, Rye (Sussex), **13**, 38
Merry Wives of Windsor, Windsor (Berks), 85
Metropolitan, Uxbridge (Middx), 69
Milecastle, Haltwhistle (Northumb), 69
Milford, Yeovil (Som), **77**, 80
Millers, Singleton (Lancs), 74
Miller of Mansfield, Goring (Oxon), 54
Miners Rest, Chasetown (Staffs), 76
Mitre, Crediton (Devon), **81**
Mitre, Tunbridge (Kent), 85
Mole, Monks Sherborne (Hants), 79
Molescroft, nr Hull (Yorks), 79
Monkey Island, Bray (Berks), 48
Monkseaton Arms, Whitley Bay (Northumb), 84
Monks Tavern, London, 19
Monument, London, 59
Moon, Wootton-under-Edge (Glos), **27**
Moonrakers, Swindon (Wilts), 54
Moorcock, Garsdale (Yorks), 79
Morris Dancers, Castleton (Derbys), 80
Moses Gate, Bolton (Lancs), 86
Mother Hubbard, Loughton (Essex), 84

Mousetrap, Bourton-on-the-Water (Glos), **89**
Mucky Duck, Gloucester (Glos), 84
Mulberry Bush, Kempston (Beds), 76
Mystery, Portsmouth (Hants), 16

Nailers, Bromsgrove (Worcs), 74
Nell Gwyne, 65
Nell of Old Drury, Drury Lane, London, 65
Nelson, 70
Nevill Arms, Astwood Bank, Redditch (Worcs), **53**
New, 87
New, Gloucester (Glos), 9, **13**, 32
New, Ross-on-Wye (Herefs), 26
New Shovels, Blackpool (Lancs), 80
Nightingale, Hitchen (Herts), 79
Nine Saxons, Reading (Berks), 48
Nineteenth Hole, Buxton (Derbys), 82
Noahs Ark, Plymouth (Devon), 62
Noahs Ark, Sheffield (Yorks), 62
Noahs Ark, St Albans (Herts), 62
Noble Art, London, NW3, 82
Nobody Inn, Doddiscombsleigh (Devon), 35
Nog Inn, 84
North London, Camden Road, London, 69
North Western, nr Stockport (Cheshire), 69
Northgate, Caerwent (Mon), **31**
Norway, Perranarworthal (Cornwall), 90

Oadby Owl, Oadby (Leics), 79
Oak & Acorn, Rosebarton (Som), 76
Oak & Ivy, Hawkhurst (Kent), 38
Odessa, 74
Old Airport, Cardiff (Glam), 80
Old Coaching House, Chudleigh (Devon), 66, **68**
Old Cock, Droitwich (Worcs), 18
Old Crown, Hayes (Middx), 86
Old Father Thames, Lambeth, London, 69
Old Hainault Oak, Hainault Forest (Essex), 87
Old House at Home, Edenbridge (Kent), 84
Old King's Head & Mermaid, London, 59
Old Maypole, Hainault (Essex), 87
Old Mint, Southam (Warks), 24
Old Peacock, Nottingham (Notts), 80
Old Roof Tree, Middleton (Lancs), 50
Old Ship, Lee-on-Solent (Hants), **49**
Old Tramway, Stratford-on-Avon (Warks), 69
Olive Branch, Canterbury (Kent), 80
Oliver Twist, Antwerp (Belgium), 95
One & Three, Oldham (Lancs), 85
Open Hearth, Scunthorpe (Lincs), 76
Orange Footman, Harlow New Town (Essex), 36
Orange Tree, Hitchen (Herts), 76

Orange Tree, Totteridge (Herts), 76
Organ, Worcester Park (Surrey), 84
Orleans Arms, Esher (Surrey), 33
Other Side of the Moon, Nottingham (Notts), 70
Owl in the Wood, Burnley (Lancs), 79
Oystermouth, Swansea (Glam), 84

'P', North London, 88
Painted Lady, Harlow New Town (Essex), 36
Panther, Reigate (Surrey), 79
Park, Exmouth (Devon), **45**
Parrot, Shalford (Surrey), 79
Parson & Clerk, Streetly (Staffs), 52
Passage House, Kingsteignton (Devon), 54
Paul Jones, Whitehaven (Cumb), 9
Paul Pry, Peterborough (Northants), 26
Paxton's Head, London, 66
Peacock, 80
Pear Tree, Charfield (Glos), **89**
Pearly Queen, Stepney, London, 48
Peldon Rose, nr Colchester (Essex), 85
Pelham, 96
Pelham, Immingham (Lincs), 61
Perseverance, Woolwich, London, 90
Pheonix, Harlow New Town (Essex), **36**, 36
Piccadilly, Paris (France), 92
Pickwick, Geneva (Switzerland), 95
Picton, Newport (Mon), 24
Pig of Lead, Bonsall (Derbys), 76
Pig of Lead, Cromford (Derbys), 76
Pilot, Exmouth (Devon), 51, **63**
Pilot Boat, 69
Piltdown Man, Maresfield (Sussex), 50
Pin Cushion, Wyberton (Lincs), 90
Pindar of Wakefield, London, 30
Pineapple, Dorney (Bucks), 76
Pineapple, Maple (Cheshire), 76
Pit Ponies, Bristol, 79
Plaisterers, Winchcombe (Glos), **73**, 74
Plough, Cold Ashton (Glos), **75**, 76
Plough, Great Munden (Herts), 24
Plough, Rusper (Sussex), **13**
Plough, Thornbury (Glos), **75**, 76
Plough & Sail, Crossbush (Sussex), 82
Polar Bear, London, WC2, 79
Poplar Kitten, Harlow New Town (Essex), 36
Poppe, Tatworth (Som), 84
Portsmouth Arms, 48
Portsmouth Arms, Umberleigh (Devon), 48
Portway, Staunton-on-Wye (Herefs), 42
Postboy, 66
Post Office, Stroud (Glos), **31**, 43
Pot of Flowers, Stowmarket (Suffolk), 90
Pride of the Forest, Bristol, 86
Prince of Teck, London, SW5, 64

Prince Regent, Stepney, East London, 88
Prinny's, Brighton (Sussex), 64
Printers, Blackburn (Lancs), 74
Proud Salopian, Shrewsbury (Salop), 80
Pub Club, Paris (France), 95
Pub Store, Paris (France), 92
Puesdown (Glos), **45**, 59
Puffing Billy, Blandford Forum (Dorset), 68
Purple Emperor, Harlow New Town (Essex), 36
Puss in Boots, Hazlewood (Derbys), 84

Quarryman's, Blackburn (Lancs), 74
Queen, Penzance (Cornwall), **15**, 64
Queen, Upper Cwmbran (Mon), **15**
Queen Adelaide, Rye (Sussex), 64
Queen & Prince Albert, London, 64
Queen Bess, Scunthorpe (Lincs), 62
Queen Edith, Cambridge (Cambs), 62
Queen Victoria, Brussels (Belgium), 95
Queen's Head, Bermondsey, London, 64
Queen's Head, Box (Wilts), 62
Queen's Head, Colney Heath (Herts), 62
Queen's Head, Lambeth, London, 64
Queen's Head, Neath (Glam), 64
Queen's Larder, Bloomsbury, London, 58
Quicksilver Mail, West Coker (Som), 66, **67**
Quiet Woman, Halstock (Dorset), 84, **89**

Rabbits, Stapleford Tawney (Essex), 86
Railway, 68
Railway, Hornchurch (Essex), 69
Railway, London, 68
Railway, Pitsea (Essex), 69
Railway, West Horndon (Essex), 69
Railway Signal, London, SE23, 69
Railway Telegraph, Forest Hill, London, 68
Railway Terminus, Bridport (Dorset), 68
Red Cow, Honiton (Devon), **75**, 79
Red Dragon, Kirkby Lonsdale (Westm), 76
Red Lion, Antwerp (Belgium), 95
Red Lion, Brussels (Belgium), 95
Red Lion, Salisbury (Wilts), 34
Red Lion, Wingham (Kent), 23
Red Rover, Barnes Common, London, 66
Rest & Welcome, Melbury Osmond (Dorset), 90
Richard Cobden, Cocking, Midhurst (W Sussex), 51
Ridgeway, Newport (Mon), **39**
Rising Moon, Matley (Cheshire), 90

Rivioli Park, Paris (France), 95
Robin Hood & Little John, Brentwood (Essex), 84
Romping Cat, Bloxwich (Staffs), 79
Rose & Crown, Croscombe (Som), **21**
Rose & Portcullis, Butleigh (Som), 62
Rothley Court, Rothley (Leics), 41
Round of Beef, Colley Gate (Worcs), 90
Roundstone, 9
Roundstone, East Preston (Sussex), 25
Rovers Return, Blackburn (Lancs), 88
Royal, Paris (France), 92
Royal, Truro (Cornwall), 32
Royal Artillery Arms, West Huntspill (Som), **71**, 72
Royal Blenheim, Oxford (Oxon), 66
Royal George, Worcester (Worcs), 30, **49**
Royal Gloucestershire Hussar, Frocester (Glos), **72**
Royal Mail, 66
Royal Marine, Combe Martin (Devon), 50
Royal Marine, Plymouth (Devon), 50
Royal Oak, 64
Royal Oak, Barking (Essex), 37
Royal Oak, Betws-y-Coed (Caern), 42
Royal Oak, Clevedon (Som), 44
Royal Oak, Gibraltar, 95
Royal Oak, Meavy (Devon), 62
Royal Oak, Wivlesfield (Sussex), 42
Royal Scot, Carlisle (Cumb), 69
Royal Yeoman, Grimstone (Dorset), **71**, 72
Rutland Arms, Newmarket (Suffolk), 56

St Germain, Paris (France), 92
St James, Paris (France), 95
St John, Blackburn (Lancs), 62
St John's, Torpoint (Devon), 62, **81**
St John of Jerusalem, London, EC1, 62
St Michel, Paris (France), 92
Salutation, 62
Same Yet, 84
Samuel Pepys, Gillingham (Kent), 90
Samuel Pepys, London, 90
Sandy Arms, Wickhamford (Worcs), 66
Satellite, Liverpool (Lancs), 70
Sawyers, Rochdale (Lancs), 74
Saye & Sele, Broughton (Oxon), 57
Scales, Lichfield (Staffs), 82
Schuman, Brussels (Belgium), 95
Sea Around Us, Loughborough (Leics), 69
Sea Horse, Gosport (Hants), 79
Sea Horse, Porthcawl (Glam), 79
Sea Horse, York (Yorks), 79
Sebastapol, 74
Sedgemoor, 96
Sedgemoor, Western Zoyland (Som), 59
Selsea Tram, Chichester (Sussex), 17

Senlac, Battle (Sussex), 74
Severn Trow, Stourport (Worcs), 69
Sexey's Arms, Blackford (Som), 26
Shark, Harlow New Town (Essex), 36
Sheaf & Sickle, Rugby (Warks), 76
Shepherd & Flock, Farnham (Surrey), 32
Shepherdess, City Road, London, 76
Shield & Dagger, Southampton (Hants), **53**
Shiny Sheff, Sheffield (Yorks), 58
Ship, Caerleon (Mon), **49**, 69
Ship, Morwellham (Devon), 44
Ship, West Croydon (Surrey), 69
Ship's Tavern & King's Head, Plymouth (Devon), **49**, 74
Shoe, Exton (Hants), 74
Short Blue, Barking (Essex), 22
Shoulder of Mutton, Oswaldtwistle (Lancs), 90
Showman, Cullompton (Devon), 55
Shrew be Shrewd, Hersden (Kent), 90
Shrimp, Morecambe (Lancs), 80
Shrimp & Turtle, Sandwich (Kent), 80
Shutter, Gotherington (Glos), **39**, 60
Silent Whistle, Evercreech (Som), 69
Silent Whistle, Oakle Street (Glos), **67**, 69
Silver Bullet, Finsbury Park, London, 69
Silver Ghost, Alveston (Derbys), 69
Silver Lion, Hitchen (Herts), 79
Silver Oyster, Colchester (Essex), 16
Simple Simon, Leamington Spa (Warks), 84
Sir John Barleycorn, Wimborne (Dorset), 85
Sir John Franklin, Poplar, London, 70
Sir Joseph Paxton, Titchfield (Hants), 66
Sir Richard Grenville, Bideford (Devon), **25**, 26
Sir William Gomm, London, SE16, 10
Sir Winston Churchill, Paris (France), 92
Sirloin, Hoghton (Lancs), 24
Sitting Goose, Bartle (Lancs), 79
Sloop, Scaynes Hill (Sussex), 18
Small Copper, Harlow New Town (Essex), 36, **37**
Smith's Arms, Godmanstone (Dorset), **87**, 87
Smugglers, Anstruther (Fife), 41
Snowcat, Cambridge (Cambs), 44
Snuff Mill, nr Bristol, 74
Soldier & Citizen, 62
South Eastern, 68
South Eastern, Tunbridge (Kent), 69
Sparrow, Letcombe Regis (Berks), 79
Spindlemakers, Preston (Lancs), 74
Spinner & Bergamot, Gt Budworth (Cheshire), 42
Spinners, Darwen (Lancs), 74

Sportsmen, Stratford-on-Avon (Warks), 82, 83
Spotted Dog, Penshurst (Kent), 79
Square Rigger, City of London, 26, 69
Squirrels Head, Gidea Park (Essex), 82
Stable Door, 66
Stag & Huntsman, Hambledon (Hants), 82
Stag Hunt, Ponsanooth (Cornwall), 82
Stag Hunters, Brendon (Som), 82
Stag's Head, Hinton Charterhouse (Som), 79
Star, Bedminster, Bristol, **81**
Star, Slad (Glos), **13**
Star, Woodstock (Oxon), 22
Star & Eagle, Goudhurst (Kent), 61
Star Castle, Isle of Scilly, 42
Star of India, Nunhead, London, 16
Steam Engine, Lambeth, London, 69
Steamer, Preston (Lancs), 69
Stock Exchange, Paris (France), 92
Stocks, Beanham (Berks), 80
Stokers, Blackburn (Lancs), 76
Stone & Faggott, Little Yeldham (Essex), 44
Stonemasons, Heywood (Lancs), 74
Student Prince, Luton (Beds), **89**
Suffolk Punch, Boreham Wood (Herts),
Suffolk Punch, Ipswich (Suffolk), 79
Sugarloaf, London, 59
Sun, Bilsdale (Yorks), 25
Sun, Bruton (Som), 26
Sun, Yeovil (Som), 26, **27**
Sun & Star, Westhill (Surrey), 90
Surrey Oaks, Newdigate (Surrey), 76
Swan, Brentwood (Essex), 52
Swan, Brussels (Belgium), 95
Swan, Coleshill (Warks), 54
Swan, Rickmansworth (Herts), 14
Swan, Yardley, Birmingham (Warks), **86**, 87
Swan & Bushes, Leicester (Leics), 79
Swan with Two Necks, London, 66
Swingletres, Callington (Cornwall), 76

Talisman, Hitchen (Herts), 90
Tanners, nr Blackburn (Lancs), 76
Tanners, Horsham (Sussex), 76
Telstar, Stockton (Co Durham), 70
Terminus, Cardiff (Glam), **67**, 82
Tern, Yate (Glos), **77**, 79
Thatchers, Great Warley (Essex), 76
The Fort St George in England, Midsummer Common (Cambs), 43
The Rock, Gibraltar, **93**, 95
The 13th Cheshire Riflemen, Stalybridge (Cheshire), 87
The Whitbread Pub, Belfort (Germany), **93**
Thomas Lord, West Meon (Hants), 65
Three Blackbirds, Bexley (Kent), 80
Three Cocks, nr Glasbury (Radnor), 30

INDEX OF INNS

Three Cups, Colchester (Essex), 16
Three Frogs, Wokingham (Berks), 80
Three Furnaces, Warley (Lancs), 76
Three Horseshoes, 66
Three Jolly Colliers, London, SE1, 74
Three Kings, Sandwich (Kent), 37
Three Lions, Godalming (Surrey), 79
Three Loggerheads, 42
Three Sugarloaves, Croydon (Surrey), 74
Three Sugarloaves, Hedingham (Essex), 74
Three Sugarloaves, Hollingbourne (Kent), 74
Three Sugarloaves, Luton (Beds), 74
Three Tuns, 76
Three Tuns, Banbury Cross (Oxon), 46
Three Willows, Birchanger (Essex), 82
Tim Bobbin, Burnley (Lancs), 54
Tim Bobbin, Rochdale (Lancs), 54
Tinker & Budget, Oswaldtwistle (Lancs), 86
Tin Mans, Forest of Dean (Glos), 76
Tinners, Blackburn (Lancs), 76
Tinners, Zennor (Cornwall), 76
Tippling, Philosopher, Grays Inn Road, London, 16
Toll Gate, 66
Tommy Ducks, Manchester (Lancs), 85
Tom Thumb, Stockport (Cheshire), 84
Top of the World, Warner's End (Herts), 88
Tower, Redhill (Surrey), 88
Traders, Mellor (Lancs), 74
Tradesmen's Arms, Stokenham (Devon), 68
Tramcar, Sheffield (Yorks), 69
Tramway, Colchester (Essex), 69
Traveller's Rest, Grasmere (Cumb), 69
Travellers Rest, Staxton (Som), **67**
Trawler, Brixham (Devon), 76
Treble Tile, West Bergholt (Essex), 74
Triangle, Rhayader (Radnor), 58
Triple Plea, Halesworth (Suffolk), 26
Trooper, Windsor (Berks), 72
Trout, Cockermouth (Cumb), 9
Trowel & Hammer, Marks Tey (Essex), 74
Trumpet Major, nr Dorchester (Dorset), 72
Tulip Tree, Richmond (Surrey), 76
Tumble Beacon, Banstead (Surrey), 90
Tumbling Sailors, Kidderminster (Worcs), 84
Turbinia, Fosseway, Newcastle-upon-Tyne (Northumb), 82
Turners, Blackburn (Lancs), 74
Turnpike, 66
Twelve Bells, Whitcombe (Glos), **81**

Twelve Knights, Port Talbot (Glam), 60
Twenty Churchwardens, Cockley Cley, Swaffham (Norfolk), 19
Twist & Cheese, Bedford (Beds), 55
Two Ships, Rochdale (Lancs), 50
Two Ships, Todmorden (Yorks), 50

Van & Horses, Uxbridge (Middlx), 68
Vauxhall, Evesham (Worcs), 59
Viaduct, Monckton Combe (Som), **31**
Victoria, Esher (Surrey), 69
Victualling Office, Plymouth (Devon), 37
Village Inn, Twyning (Glos), **31**
Vine, 76
Virginia Ash, Henstridge (Som), **63**
Volunteer, Lyme Regis (Dorset), **71**, 74
Volunteer, Seavington (Som), **71**, 74

Waggon & Horses, Belsay (Northumb), 68
Waggon & Horses, Birchanger (Essex), 82
Waggon & Horses, Glastonbury (Som), **75**
Waggonmakers, Bury (Lancs), 74
Wait for the Waggon, Wyboston (Beds), 66
Wake, nr Epping (Essex), 23
Walnut Tree, Ditton (Kent), 76
Walnut Tree, Matfield (Kent), 76
Walnut Tree, Pyle (Glam), 76
Walpole, Blackburn (Lancs), 65
Walrus, 10
Warren, Romney (Kent), 80
Wat Tyler, Middlesbrough (Yorks), 65
Waterloo, nr Taddington (Derbys), 70
Waterloo House, Bridgwater (Som), **63**, 70, **99**
Wayfarer, Bristol, 69
Weighbridge, Longford (Glos), **89**
Wellington, Dusseldorf (Germany), **93**, 95
Wellington Arms, Rorks Bridge (Som), 70
Whately Hall, Banbury (Oxon), 47
Wheelbarrow, Southsea Common (Hants), 24
Whiffler, Norwich (Norfolk), 80
Whip & Saddle, Duns (Berwicks), 82
Whistling Duck, nr Weston-super-Mare (Som), **43**, 43
White Admiral, Harlow New Town (Essex), 36
White Bear, Bedale (Yorks), 85
White Boar, Bury (Lancs), 79
White Hart, Biggin Hill (Kent), 48
White Hart, Cinderford (Glos), **78**
White Hart, Yetminster (Dorset), 79
White Horse, Chilham (Kent), 61
White Horse, Wallington (Hants), **78**
White Horse Cellar, Piccadilly, London, 66
Whitesmiths Arms, Gloucester

(Glos), **73**, 74
Whitesmiths, Wigan (Lancs), 74
White Swan, Henley-in-Arden (Warks), 54
White Swan, Woodnewton (Northants), 46
Whoop Hall, nr Settle (Yorks), 33
Wicor Mill, Portchester (Hants), **39**, 80
Widow's Son, Bow, London, 50
Wig & Fidgett, Boxstead (Essex), 12
Wild Boar, Congleton (Staffs), 84
Wild Duck, Ewen (Glos), 80
Wild Duck, nr Peterborough (Northants), 80
William IV, Shepton Mallet (Som), **15**, 64
William IV, Tunley (Som), 64
Willow Beauty, Harlow New Town (Essex), 36
Winkle, Basingstoke (Hants), 80
Winston & Kipling, Brussels (Belgium), 95
Woodcock, Hindhead (Surrey), 80
Woodbine, Epping Forest (Essex), 87
Woodin's Shades, Bishopsgate, London, 33
Woodmans, Black Fen (Kent), 74
Woodmans, Halstead (Essex), 74
Woodmans, Newcastle-upon-Tyne (Northumb), 74
Wool Pack, 80
Wool Pack, nr Weston-super-Mare (Som), **21**, 80
World's End, Ecton (Northants), 26
World's End, Knaresborough (Yorks), 26
Wrestlers, Cambridge (Cambs), 82
Wych Way, Brockhurst (Hants), 84

Yarn Spinners, Spondon (Derbys), 74
Yellow Rose, Middlesbrough (Yorks), 76
Ye Olde Bell, Rye (Sussex), 38
Ye Olde Cheshire Cheese, Fleet Street, London, 33
Ye Olde Cross, Alnwick (Northumb), 20
Ye Olde London, London, 80
Ye Olde Pipemakers, Rye (Sussex), 74
Ye Olde Tippling Philosopher, 87
Ye Olde Tippling Philosopher, Caldicot (Mon), 16
Ye Olde Tudor, Dusseldorf (Germany), **93**, 95
Yeoman, Gloucester (Glos), 71
York Arms, Ghent (Belgium), 95
York Minster, Soho, London, 29
Yorkshire Terrier, Brinsworth (Yorks), 57
Young Vanish, Chesterfield (Derbys), 61, **83**
Yuticks' Nest, Blackburn (Lancs), 11

Zebra, Cambridge (Cambs), 79
Zulu, Ipswich (Suffolk), 74